Small Town Girl

For Saoirse and Rosa

Small Town Girl

Donna McLean

HODDER*studio*

First published in Great Britain in 2022 by Hodder Studio
An Imprint of Hodder & Stoughton
An Hachette UK company

2

A CIP catalogue record for this title is available from the British Library

Hardback ISBN 9781529379853
eBook ISBN 9781529379860

Typeset in Sabon MT by Hewer Text UK Ltd, Edinburgh
Printed and bound in Great Britain by Clays Ltd, Elcograf S.p.A.

Hodder & Stoughton policy is to use papers that are natural, renewable
and recyclable products and made from wood grown in sustainable
forests. The logging and manufacturing processes are expected to
conform to the environmental regulations of the country of origin.

Hodder & Stoughton Ltd
Carmelite House
50 Victoria Embankment
London EC4Y 0DZ

www.hodder-studio.com

Prologue

Ramping up speed as we left north London behind. Burning along country roads on the sleek black Suzuki. He always drove fast, even in the estate car. He borrowed the cash for his new toy from work, paying it back out of his wages. He bought me all the gear: tight-fitting jacket, gloves, shiny black helmet.

'You look the part,' he said.

'You're a speed junky,' I teased.

'I don't touch drugs. My vices are fast bikes and fierce women.'

'*Women*?!' Mock indignation.

'Just you, and Suzi.'

'You love that bike more than me!'

'I love you, darlin'. More than you'll ever know.'

My hair blowing out from under the motorbike helmet. It was getting long again and he wanted me to grow it. He liked it when I wore the things he bought me too: huge hoop earrings, long boots, dresses above the knee, designer sunglasses. He was generous.

A traditional working-class Italian boy.

We drove further into the countryside north of London and he knew all the roads. 'From when I was working at the locksmith's, darlin'. I did a lot of work in these posh houses.'

He pulled in beside a shady thicket, kicked down the bike stand. Turning to face me, he lifted his visor and gestured at me to raise mine. I fumbled, still clumsy, not used to my new uniform. He raised it for me, delicately, big hands gentler than they looked.

'Shall we?'

Those eyes. He pulled me towards the darkness of the trees and started unzipping my leather jacket. We were moments from a busy road, but I didn't care. I never cared; he could have led me over a cliff edge if he'd wanted to.

Out of the Blue

July 2015

> Hey D, it's Den here. Hope you're well? Can we talk?
> About Carlo? Sorry if this is a bit out of the blue . . .

The Facebook message pops up on my phone and reading it makes me feel sick. Something looming, a heaviness in my stomach. Dizzy. Clammy. Eyes blur. Tingling, in my fingers and my toes. A tiny bit of sick comes up. Shivering suddenly, I reach for my green fluffy cardigan, which I have only just removed. The basement is stiflingly hot, as usual. The anxiety group had forgotten to turn off the heating.

I am about to facilitate my weekly mental health support group, a particularly high-octane gang of rebels and outsiders. I always stipulate that I have the final say on referrals to my programme, so make a point of accepting people with seeming complexity, often rejected or failed by other services. I have two unbendable rules – no active suicidality and no recent bereavements. It's unsafe to work with certain risk factors in a community-group setting, although I have worked with those clients many times in the past. I have undergone proper training and I have over twenty years of experience working in the field. Several of my current clients have borderline personality disorder (BPD), there are two with the mood disorder cyclothymia, three dual diagnoses, two with autism spectrum disorder (ASD) and one adult with attention deficit hyperactivity disorder (ADHD), newly diagnosed.

It makes me edgy, reading tricky texts or emails before a session. It is all about creating the right psychological space so I can hold whatever big emotions or memories might arise in the session. I mentally kick myself. *You must not read messages just before group! Repeat this mantra, you fool.*

Too late. I now have precisely five minutes to restore myself and prepare the room for my session. It has been left in a heap by the group who were in earlier. They never wash up their mugs. There is a pile of squashed teabags left to fester, staining the sink rust-brown. And the bin is similarly stagnant, emitting a sweet and sickly scent, overflowing with used tissues, apple cores and banana skins.

Helplessly, my mind is pulled back to the message, and Dennis. He lives close to me now, a little further along the Kent coast, near Margate, in a cottage surrounded by flowers and plants. It's a far cry from the lawless council estate in Hackney where I first met him in 2002. Carlo and I helped him move from there to a red-brick flat on the Peabody estate set back from the frenetic Old Kent Road. The three of us had shifted Den's boxes of books and art materials up five flights of Victorian tenement stairs – the perils of inner-city living. Carlo had been the driver, of course, and he did most of the heavy lifting too. He was built like a bull.

Three years later, Dennis had reciprocated, helping when I moved from a friend's sofa in Camberwell to a sublet at the top of Brixton Hill. There was no Carlo to do the hard graft that time, just Den, Tania and me. Barely a practical bone between us, and none of Carlo's muscle. It was one of many moves during those restless London years and Mum still complains about the mess I've made of her address book, each of my temporary stops scratched out in frustrated blue ink.

Dennis lives with an artist now and it seems they are equally reclusive. We reconnected on Facebook via a mutual contact in Folkestone, where I had moved in 2012. Den and I had known each other well back in the London days and he'd had a bit of a soft spot for me – was always happy to whip me up a decent spaghetti puttanesca after helping with my umpteenth house move.

I catch myself drifting away into a strangely pleasant nostalgia, so I drag myself back to the here and now. I must focus on my group, so I go to punch out a hasty reply. It's all about the tone, and I feel pressured to say the right thing. As I read his message again, my jaw tightens at the implication of his request. Try to unclench it. Words. Just type words. Keep it simple. *Keep it flat.* I close my eyes for a few seconds and push my energy down to my feet on the ground, willing it away from the anxious zone around my chest and belly. *Focus.* I open my eyes and come back to the boiling-hot room. I type efficiently:

Hi Den, good to hear from you. Yep, all good here! Busy as usual . . . work/ kids. In work now, but happy to talk after 8.30 p.m.? D xx

Kisses, so not a hostile response. Tone. Keeping it all perfectly casual. But I feel like someone has sucked all the energy from me and it's only a few minutes until my clients are due to arrive. They are an unusually punctual group. I force myself to silence the phone and shove it deep into the front pocket of my rucksack; zip it up, put it away. Hide it.

'Fuck off.' My voice is a low, venomous whisper.

I glare at the bulging bag, warning it not to distract me for the entire two-hour session. I look up to the door opening and my first group member walking into the room. She's early, which is revealing in itself.

'Hi, Donna! How are you, my darling?'

'Hiya, Jenny. Good, thanks, the kettle's just on. How's your week been?'

Jenny is a reliable group member. I can tell she is elated by the tone of her voice and when I turn from the sink to face her, I can see from her make-up, hair and clothes that we are in for a lively session. When Jenny is becoming unwell, she wears bright green eyeshadow and backcombs her silver hair to Amy Winehouse heights. She still looks fabulous though. Great cheekbones.

'Not slept a wink, Donna. Work, work, work . . .! I've got a show coming up and I'm painting all through the night to get it finished. Eight canvases. Those bloody neighbours are off again, complaining about the noise, it's been so stressful this week. They are *so* unreasonable. We can't all work nine to five like a bunch of robots!'

Jenny plays loud music – stylistically varying from Dusty Springfield to N.W.A. – while she paints, regardless of the hour. She lives in a basement flat in one of the grand but faded Georgian terraces near the seafront. A young couple, down from London and about to have their first baby, have recently moved into the flat upstairs. The harbour area is regenerating at a furious pace and the DFLs are arriving en masse, accompanied by lorryloads of Apple Macs, Eames chairs, Formica tables and KitchenAid blenders. They are decent folk, and tolerant up to a point.

'How did you get on with seeing Mick this week?' Mick is Jenny's community psychiatric nurse. He's cute, Irish and plays in a band. He's a good one, conscientious, unlike some I've come across.

'Mick's a *complete* bastard.'

I surmise from this that Mick has mentioned – gently – that Jenny's mood is on the upswing again, a fact Jenny does not want to acknowledge. This segment of the cyclothymia cycle is great fun. Life is vibrant and the colours are bright, the music tunefully loud, and the paint jumps right onto the canvas with a rhythm all its own. If only the hand stayed put, right there. Unfortunately, it will swing further upwards, almost to the point of mania. Jenny will then spend money she doesn't have, drink way too much and take different strangers home. This might go on for a week or two, and then her mood will drop, plummeting to a depressive slump. Jenny might not turn up for a few weeks after today's group, and next time she might be dressed in black or navy, no make-up, hair scraped back in a severe ponytail, face pale and eyes shameful.

The other group members drift in, not all carrying the same energy as Jenny. We have a full house. I am thrilled that Stephen has returned. It's the fourth week of eight and he's missed two, which is the maximum I can allow in order for people to graduate from the programme. Stephen has been passed from pillar to post his entire life. Care, prison, drugs, street, hostels. The system says he's untreatable and he feels unlovable. I tell him he is worthy of love, that we all are. If we can start to drop the shame we carry around like a sack of stones, we have an opportunity to change, to flourish. I'd watched him start to open up in the group over the first couple of weeks, and I desperately wanted him to go the distance. He takes his headphones out now and his hands don't shake quite as much as usual. Then he allows his black hood to come down, so we can see his face. It shows his scars, internal and external.

When the group is over, I allow myself a moment of happiness before Den's message forces its way back into my head. I didn't think about it, or Carlo, while the group was in session. I'm pleased with myself for remaining focused. I stretch back in the battered dining chair, arms above my head in a yoga pose, taking a deep breath, allowing a ghost of a smile. *Well done. Well bloody done.*

I'd written my new group exercises with a deliberate emphasis on values and self-compassion, which makes the sessions more effective for those with anxiety, depression and stress. The changes were well received by the participants, though I had trialled the whole-group programme on myself before letting it loose on the clients, with a genuine interest in self-discovery I had completed a five-day boot camp in Acceptance and Commitment Therapy a few months before, during the Easter holidays. As a result,. I introduced the ACT Values Bullseye, which not only helps clarify what your values are, but places them on a bullseye graphic to determine how closely you're living your life by your values and where there are areas for cultivation. I learned that work and education were my core priorities, but the areas of health and relationships were lacking direction. I questioned my relationships most of all. I'd moved from London without knowing anyone in this town. I travelled a lot for work, so couldn't meet people that way, and my time at home was focused on the children. I felt guilty if I went out in the evenings. Life wasn't exactly bad, but it felt like there was something missing. The connected, social part of me felt subdued. I had made notes on the edge of my bullseye.

Meet like-minded people!
Join a group ... maybe?
Go to events. Politics? Get involved?

During the ACT course, I stayed in London with Iain, an old friend and the brother of The Artist, an ex from my 20s. We'd had one of those priceless times that you can only have with old mates, reminiscing, listening to Warren Zevon and Johnny Cash and drinking twenty-five-year-old malt whisky until three in the morning. I gave myself permission to be reckless because the kids were with their dad, and Iain's girlfriend was back in New Zealand for a month. She didn't approve of our late-night shenanigans, so her absence, and the whisky, had fuelled our hedonism. On the last night of the course, my final evening of freedom, Iain and I found ourselves sitting at his kitchen table. We were both tired from the week and reminiscing on the rose-tinted stamina of the old days.

'Do you remember that Burns Night party where your leather jacket was robbed?'

'Aye.' Iain still looked annoyed, years later. 'That prick Dennis. Stole my MiniDisc player as well.'

'Well, he only meant to take the jacket. He was cold, bless him, and all upset with the world. His girlfriend had left him. He was remorseful the next day, do you remember? Shamefaced!'

'Aye, it was Carlo who sorted it out. Where is that fat prick these days, any idea?'

It was the first time I'd heard Carlo's name in years. His face pushed into my thoughts and I tried to shove it back out, to stay in the room.

'Who? Carlo? Or Den?' I wanted more than anything to stay casual.

'Carlo. Dennis was a skinny fucker.'

'Christ knows where Carlo is. Last I heard of him was in 2006! At Tania's fortieth. I bumped into someone he went to football matches with. He'd heard that Carlo moved back to Italy. And he'd had an accident – fell off his Ducati . . .'

'Serves him right. I can't believe how he treated you.'

I glared at Iain. I didn't want our nostalgic bubble to be pierced by bad memories. 'So you think his behaviour worse than your brother's? Really?'

Iain ignored this. He worshipped his older brother, The Artist. He also still felt hellishly guilty, all these years later. He had known all about the affair with the actress, but didn't tell me, even as his brother was calling me a paranoid lunatic. At the time this wounded me, another deep, painful betrayal. Iain and I had been friends for twenty years, introduced by a teacher who recognised our talents as painters, independently of me meeting The Artist. Blood is thicker than water I suppose.

'And what about Dennis? Do you still keep in touch with him?'

'Den is – believe it or not – living down the road from me now, in sunny Kent of all places. With a photographer. He's as quiet as a mouse these days. They've got a few rescue cats, but no kids.'

'Aye? Sounds like the perfect life.'

Iain wasn't remotely envious of my domestic life; kids and dogs and mess and juggling freelance work and travel. I loved the busyness of the world I'd created. Life wasn't perfect, but in my forties I felt that I was finally finding my place in the world. It hadn't always been that way; a twenties spent counselling had left me feeling a frequent despair, too enmeshed in the troubles of other people. But abandoning it for a career as a team manager in homelessness and drug treatment services had disconnected me from the world, and having children slightly later than planned and getting seriously ill at the age of forty had invited me to throw everything up in the air. As soon as my babies were born, I had felt claustrophobic in London, magnified by the difficulty of making 'mum friends'. Restless as always, I'd uprooted us to France for a year, figuring it was the best use of my extended maternity leave. I was glad I had twins. It meant I could break the rules, ignore the yummy-mummy clubs and gastropub get-togethers. My family were far away in Scotland and most of my London friends didn't have kids, or they had grown up and fled the nest. I morphed into a machine of motherhood, first breastfeeding and then making my own baby food with quinoa and mashed avocado. It was just me and the girls, me and them in the double buggy, chasing the old dog round the park when it stole baguettes from the picnickers.

The first two years parenting twins was tiring but I felt the strongest sense of purpose I had ever experienced. I returned to work full time when they were two and a half, to take on the most full-on, demanding job an exhausted mum of two toddlers could possibly consider. Everyone thought I was mad. At the job interview, a snooty man in a suit said my predecessor had fled to Afghanistan (to work for the UN) to escape the hell of managing the drug and alcohol treatment services in Woolwich.

I turned the place upside down. Broke the hierarchy. Implemented changes. I insisted on fresh flowers from the market in reception and bowls of fruit scattered around the communal areas. I insisted on art in the therapy rooms. One of my managers was belligerent; it would be a distraction, he said, from the treatment. No, I said, it would show people we care about them. I won the clients and the staff round. I almost broke my body and my spirit in the process. One day, just before Christmas 2011, I collapsed. Literally gave way – my body said no. Dealing with a more-than-full-time job, two small people and a difficult relationship took all the wind from my sails and (temporarily) all the movement from my arms and legs.

I recovered slightly, went back to work part time for a few months, determined to finish the task I'd set myself. We were almost there. The once failing service was now a go-to for new managers. A beacon of positive practice. A year before we'd had a frighteningly long waiting list for alcohol detoxes that included three people who were dead. Now we had a thriving group work programme, support for family and friends, a peer support training package and fresh flowers twice a week. I lasted until the following Christmas, 2012, then had to accept defeat. I had a yet to be diagnosed auto-immune disease and my instinct was to get out of London and head for the seaside.

It was training as a mindfulness teacher, an ACT therapist, that reconnected me to some sense of meaning. A role, and one that I understood inside and out. My life now is two girls under ten and all that entails, trips to conferences and training, and this basement room. These groups, and all that comes with them.

Locking up the basement of the mental health service, alarm set, lights off. Doing everything on autopilot. Outside in the still-warm night, breathing in the salt of the sea. Looking up at the sky and black clouds were washing in from France. Red sky at night, shepherd's delight. Red sky in the morning, shepherd's warning. We were due a storm, to break the stifling heat, and the tightness of the atmosphere extended to my head, jaw and neck. Memories kept pushing in; Den's text knocking against thoughts that I'd buried long ago.

I thought of my friend Tania, who had visited a few weeks earlier. Tania had sold her flat in London and moved back to Scotland two years earlier, making the best of a relationship gone tits-up and a sharp increase in the house prices in the south-east.

She found the south-coast heat unbearable.

'Sweating like a bastard here – how do you put up with it? You're more Celtic than me.'

She was half Glaswegian-Irish, half Sicilian, with jet-black hair styled in a neat bob. Her skin was pale as porcelain.

'Linen, factor fifty and a big hat, doll.'

We had a day out, drinking pints of ice-cold Spanish lager and eating tapas in a shady beer garden while the kids were at school.

Later that evening, rocking back and forth on my Bentwood chair in the attic, which doubled as spare room and my office, Tania yelped and lurched for her handbag. The rocking chair nearly tipped upright, knocking over the bottle of red wine, which I caught in slow motion.

'While I remember, you have GOT to read this.' She shoved a book towards me. I took it, looking at the cover. A masked face, like the Anonymous group. *Undercover*, by Rob Evans, who I knew was a *Guardian* journalist. He had been covering the so-called 'spycops' story, about undercover policemen who had duped female activists into relationships, posing as environmental campaigners and socialists.

I'd first read about the story in the *Observer* back in 2010, when an undercover policeman revealed how he infiltrated anti-racist activist groups. He recounted the bizarre double life he had led, the psychological stress it had caused and his growing worry that the work of his secret unit could threaten people's right to legitimate protest.

One by one, the undercover spies had had their covers blown by activists. First Mark Kennedy in 2010, who infiltrated a group of environmental activists and was exposed by Lisa, his then partner, then Bob Lambert, who was accused of planting a bomb in a Debenhams store in London in 1987 to prove his commitment to animal rights. Lambert even had a child with an activist, before disappearing from their lives.

In 2014, I had watched a Channel 4 *Dispatches* programme that delved further into the scandal. It featured the same police whistle-blower, Peter Francis, who had by now dropped his anonymity. Three women who had been deceived into long-term relationships (Helen Steel, Jacqui and Belinda) were also interviewed.

That same year, I'd watched an interview on BBC *Newsnight* with a woman called 'Alison' who didn't show her face on the TV. I remembered her slim hands and expensive leather belt threaded through blue jeans. She was part of a group of eight women who brought the first case against the Metropolitan Police for human rights abuses in 2011. They were still fighting their cases.

I'd found myself compulsively watching these interviews, eyes glued to the screen. Having spent my life invested in the people most impacted by injustice, I felt a deep pang for these women so mistreated by the system. They looked like my old friends, the passionate and energetic friends I'd marched with, who'd each followed different threads from that same starting point. Watching these women talk, I missed my youth. I felt deeply angry, and I couldn't look away, burning in sympathy for these strangers and their strange, awful situation. Obviously, Tania felt the same way.

'It's unbelievable, what them fuckers did! They infiltrated the Socialist Party, did you know that? And the Stephen Lawrence campaign. They spied on his family and deliberately let the wee bastard fascists that killed him get away with it! That big fella, Pete Francis, it turns out he was an undercover cop . . . Did you ever meet him on demos? He was known as Pete Black, with the south-London lot, YRE. Bit mad looking, starey eyes, liked a bit of a ruck?'

I shook my head no. 'The YRE? Who are they?'

'The Socialists!' Tania believes I lack a proper political education. (She's fundamentally right).

'I'll have a read of it now.'

After a glass of wine, Tania began falling asleep in the chair. At this time of night, with the kids in bed, the attic became a peaceful space, wall-to-wall with dusty books and my favourite print of the UCS Glasgow shipbuilders sit-in by Ken Currie, skilfully framed by Iain, in the prime spot above my desk.

I gently nudged her shoulder, causing her to jump.

'Time for bed,' I whispered, guiding her up from the chair by her elbow, over to the futon in the corner, under the eaves. 'Watch your head.'

I left clean towels for the morning on the chair beside her and crept downstairs, past the kids' room, clutching the *Undercover* book and the half a bottle of Rioja that I rescued from spillage. The book was intriguing and discomforting, awakening a niggling doubt I had about the past. That episode in London that I'd tried to keep locked away for so long.

I read the book straight through that night. The next morning, over strong black coffee, we talked about the book in detail. It was a conversation that stretched from the political into the deeply personal, and we clasped each other's hands as we thought about our own pasts.

Tania and I had both grown up in the west of Scotland, working-class, passionate about politics and music. We both had single mothers and Irish heritage. We were both deeply connected to our friends, loyal to the core. We'd both wanted to go to art school but didn't quite make it. We loved Scotland but had both escaped, for different reasons. We knew many of the same people, but our paths only crossed in 2004 when Tania came to work in Camberwell, south London, for the same organisation as me, her managing mental health and me managing the substance misuse team.

Tania was instantly suspicious of there being another gobby Scottish cow in the office, but we soon bonded over a shared love of David Bowie and the Brian Jonestown Massacre. She became my gig buddy, my confidante, her house my spare-couch stopover when I couldn't face going home.

'A lot of good times too though. Remember the time we went to Granada and Tony fell out with us all and disappeared for two days? Turned out he'd been up in a helicopter, sightseeing over the Alhambra? We'd been worried sick.'

'Maniac,' we said simultaneously, laughing at the ridiculousness of it all.

'You have to enjoy the good bits, and the memories,' she said. 'You'll get eaten up with fear and rage otherwise.'

'I won't let them destroy me like that.'

Once Tania returned to Glasgow, I read *Undercover* again, sifting out intricate details of undercover operations. I wasn't quite sure why; I just had an urge to understand this story. When I got the text message from Den, something clicked and my interest became personal, not just political.

Now, sitting in my kitchen, door closed, I type Den's number into the phone.

2

The Reunion

Den doesn't answer my call. Instead, a few minutes later, a shrill beep makes me jump.

> Dan, Liam and Outreach Joe are meeting Dave Blacklist on Tuesday night. London KX. Meet at Housmans bookshop at 6.30 p.m. Can you make it? Dx

I'm not surprised he doesn't have the courage yet to speak to me directly, but this group of names tells me everything I need to know.

Dan. One of my closest friends for a few years. We did the *Guardian* crossword every day on our lunchbreak in our sticky office above the fish shop in Camberwell. I bought the Socialist Party newspaper from him, to humour him. We both agreed that LBC was the best radio station and Robert Elms the best DJ, though he was alone in his love for West Ham and Billy Bragg. He knew London like the back of his hand and decided on the venues for all our work nights out. Our team of homelessness and addiction workers had a lively social life in the early 2000s. We would regularly have Friday nights out, starting in a pub in Soho or Camden, always chosen by Dan. Then on to a restaurant, again chosen by Dan. He was like a London cabbie: knew every backstreet. He brought homemade arancini for lunch, and always shared. 'Fancy,' I'd say, and he'd blush.

He had been absent from my life for ten years. He didn't want to see much of me after Carlo left and the thought of seeing him in the flesh brings up shame.

Liam. Liam the builder. Scouser, stocky, successful, generous. Sharp edges, but soft heart. When I looked round at moments in my life, Liam would be there, always at the heart of the group. He took everything in, cared for all of us, though he'd never say it. Not long after I'd met Carlo we'd ended up crammed onto a long table in a Japanese restaurant near our favourite dark, old pub in Shepherd Market. A dozen friends, elbow to elbow, laughing and arguing about the day we'd had. My eyes were locked on Carlo's when Liam slapped me round the head.

'What the hell are you doing?!'

'Your hair's on fire, D!'

They all laughed. One of my loose, messy bunches had strayed into the candle flame. I could smell it. Liam stayed out with us that evening, dancing and chatting in a bar in Islington until closing time. Finally, Carlo came home with me.

Outreach Joe. I first met Joe on a 'managing in the voluntary sector' training course in Holloway.

'You look like a friend of mine,' I'd said, as we paired up for a role-play exercise in how to supervise staff.

'Which friend is that?'

'Dan?'

'Dan was my best man!'

'No way! What a coincidence!'

'Yeah! Oh, it was a great day. Informal, but lovely. We had the Proclaimers as our first dance, "500 Miles".'

'I once served the Proclaimers in the Indian restaurant I worked in when I was a kid. The Taj, it was called. They were lovely.'

We'd spent the rest of the course as conspirators, gossiping in the corner, having lunch together. We'd go to the pub with Dan sometimes, but we never got that close. Joe's wife hates me. Carlo told me that.

Dave Blacklist. Not met him before. A quick Google search tells me he's a prominent trade union activist and founder of the Blacklist Support Group. I pore over websites and Twitter feeds for information, a clue as to why I'm meeting him. Everyone seems to love him, except the bosses and the cops.

This meeting is five days away, but it's making me sick already. And then there's the location.

Housmans Bookshop in King's Cross. Housmans is legendary. Not just a workers' collective-owned radical bookshop, but also a meeting place, home to several activist groups.

I'd been there before, with Carlo. To buy Joe a birthday present, perhaps? I had arranged to meet Carlo after work, as I'd been to a meeting at Camden Town Hall. It was too late to travel back to the office in Camberwell, so I finished work early. Carlo was still at Franchi's Locksmiths then and I'd texted him, said I was free and to make an excuse to come and meet me. We can't have been together long, maybe two months. Still in the first throes, seeing each other at any opportunity, clinging onto each other in supermarkets and staying in bed all Saturday afternoon.

Alongside socialist literature, Housmans stocks radical gifts for any occasion, everything from stationery to mugs with political slogans. Carlo bought a pack of Christmas cards, to distribute with edible gifts at the festive party Dan hosted for the gang, and a tea towel that caught my eye. A favourite William Morris design, the Strawberry Thief. That was before the trouble started, so it must have been before 2004. It was an afternoon spent in a haze of bliss, moving through the aisles, browsing political books before getting the tube back to Maida Vale together, where Carlo would cook dinner. Involtini, green salad dressed with apple cider vinegar and lemon and a crisp Riesling to accompany. I would neatly set the table and choose the music.

I never made it to Dan's pre-Christmas do as I had hurt my back and couldn't face it. I persuaded Carlo to go without me but ended up getting a taxi to A&E while he was out. Of course, I couldn't stop myself texting him, telling him where I was, how many hours into the queue. He came to find me straight from the party, eyes filled with concern.

We were both travelling the next day, him to Italy and me to Scotland, and we were worried I might not make it, but the doctor had studied medicine in Edinburgh and was determined to get me home for Christmas. He duly topped me up with diazepam and codeine, and gave me extra for the journey.

Carlo had come into the room pushing a wheelchair in front of him. 'Your carriage awaits, ma'am,' he'd said, winking at me. He'd raced me down the corridors, commentating on the speed and each room we'd whistled past. And he'd carried me up two flights of stairs to my flat, heavy-breathing at the top, but he made it over the threshold before dropping me onto the sofa.

That evening he'd treated me like an invalid, over-egging the role for effect, and I'd laughed along. But he'd been quiet too, tapping his fingers on the table as we watched the TV.

'What's up, love?' I'd asked, more than once, and he'd just shaken his head. I knew from a few comments that he wasn't looking forward to seeing his father in Italy, but I didn't know more than that. I didn't ask. A typical man – early thirties and still can't talk about family pain.

The morning after Carlo drove me to the airport and walked me to Departures, looping his arm through mine and guiding me and my suitcase through the holiday crowds.

'I wish we were spending Christmas together,' he'd said, as he held me at the departure gate. He sounded so unusually miserable, but I wanted to hold onto his words. To keep them. He hugged me close, more softly than usual, wary of my injured back.

'Don't worry, my love, I'll be fine. We'll be together again in a week. Next year we'll have Christmas together.'

'I have no doubt about that, my darlin'.'

I wrote Christmas cards on the plane, the small cheerful cards from Housmans. I'd wanted to send one to him, but he hadn't given me his address in Italy.

Housmans Bookshop. This Thursday night. I have to go.

By lunchtime the day of the meeting I've spent twenty minutes at the kitchen table staring out of the window. Before I become overwhelmed, I try to work things out: collect kids from school at 3.15 p.m. Home by 3.30 p.m. No chatting at the gate today. Feed the dogs, feed the kids, walk the dogs.

Outfit: smart, petrol-coloured linen trousers, fitted linen jacket with the antique thistle brooch the children bought me, a long-sleeved top in muted grey, a splash of red on my scarf.

Leave the house at 4.45 p.m. in time to catch the 5 p.m. train to London. It's a six-minute walk from the platform at St Pancras to Housmans. I've checked three times on Google Maps.

The train is almost empty. Everyone is travelling in the other direction, commuting home from a day's graft in London. It's a warm evening and the air conditioning is on. My eyes start to water as soon as I sit down and I realise that going heavy on the eye make-up was a bad move today.

I have my headphones on and am listening to a Spotify playlist I made especially for travelling. Stompy, pacey music. For walking with boots and a backpack, not travelling to meetings with a group of men you haven't seen in ten years or don't know at all. It isn't right, this music. I scroll through my many playlists, agitated. Each one transports me back to the place I made it for. Paris, London, Glasgow, Sicily.

'Bella Ciao' is in a London playlist, but it shouldn't be. That left-wing anthem belongs to Bologna. A vivid memory. 2003. A band playing in a cave-like bar, revolutionary posters with tattered edges lining the stone walls. Dancing close to you, your torso solid behind me, red T-shirt drenched in sweat, huge arms around my waist. Safe. I make a new playlist, adding 'Bella Ciao', by the Modena City Ramblers and Goran Bregovic. I have another sharp, noisy memory of Goran Bregovic and his brass band at the Barbican. Your large hand encircling my fishnetted knee. I give the playlist a title. TSWNLM. *The Spy Who Never Loved Me*. I start adding to it.

'You Are Everything', Marvin Gaye, September 2002, on our first morning together, our first breakfast in bed. My flat in Maida Vale, the sun streaming in the bedroom window. We woke up at the same time. Not shy at our nakedness. It didn't feel vulnerable, it felt right. I asked if you wanted to go for breakfast.

'Stay in bed, darlin',' you'd said. 'I'll cook.'

You went to the corner shop and found the ingredients to make a perfect hollandaise sauce from scratch. You asked where the coffee maker was. 'I don't have one,' I said, just slightly shamed.

'Instant?' You laughed. 'I'm gonna buy you a Moka pot. You'll never drink instant again.' You were right on that count.

We ate your eggs Benedict sprawled on the bed, Sunday broadsheets spread out on top of the sheets, and music floating out of the radio. It would have made a perfect scene for Instagram, had it been around then. We pretended to read the *Guardian* and *La Repubblica* (it was Maida Vale after all), then crawled back under the covers for another few hours.

'Iris', the Goo Goo Dolls. 2003 and we were six months into the relationship. Rick Stein's for dinner, our first evening in Padstow. Sea bass, of course, and a bottle of chilled, crisp Vermentino. We had the biggest room, while Dan and Kate were just down the corridor. This was our second trip to Cornwall with them, a break for Kate, whose mum was in a nursing home. It was a tough slog for them to visit, not having a car, and you offered to drive them, in the black estate car. It was longer than getting to Scotland. You barely knew Kate. I loved your kindness.

In bed that night you recited the words to the song, and you held me too tight and you cried. 'We won't last more than two years – nothing ever lasts more than two years.'

I got angry with you.

'Don't mess me around, Carlo. I've been through enough. You know that.'

'I'm scared it won't work. It's always complicated.'

'You can leave right now if that's what you think. I'm not in this for a fling.' I extracted myself from the covers, angrily pulling a Che Guevara T-shirt down over my head. I felt shamefully exposed.

'No, I'm not going anywhere. I'll always love you, darlin'. No matter what happens. I'll always love you.'

I believed every word that you said.

'Dry Your Eyes', the Streets. Crossing the river in the blue estate car, moving my stuff to Steve's place in 2004. Feeling sick with shame at my failure. Failure to provide for myself, failure to save our relationship. Tears flowing through Camberwell, yours and mine. Winding past my office in Denmark Hill, the Joiners Arms and the Maudsley. All these familiar places that I didn't want to see. My life was going backwards. You were moving in with Steve Hedley, so everyone in the group would know I had failed to keep you. My love wasn't enough to keep you safe from harm.

The train journey to London passes in a cloyingly nostalgic blur.

My feet somehow find their way off the train and I snake my way down the platform. The station is packed with people waiting to escape the stifling heat and bustle of the city. I knock into a woman holding two mini gin and tonics from M&S. She glares at me.

'Sorry!' I mouth to her, head turning just enough to see her dry, pursed lips. I'm heading straight for the toilet, stomach cramping, waves of sweat and nausea working against me.

That face in the mirror is not me. Red eyes, straggly hair, blotchy neck. Not me. I grab my make-up bag, pushing my hair back with my sunglasses. I squeeze a spot of foundation out of the tube, but too much sputters out and small, messy particles fly onto my jacket. Like a bloodstain pattern.

'Fuck!' I extract a baby wipe from my bag and rub at the stain, but it only gets bigger.

'Try a little bit of hand soap, love,' says the kind-faced woman who is cleaning the toilets. 'Here, I'll show you.'

She puts a sliver of soap from the dispenser onto her fingertip, mixing it with water, then massages the stain with a clean cloth until it becomes a dark wet circle rather than a beige blob. She guides me over to the hand-dryer and holds my jacket underneath for a couple of blasts.

'There you go, love, all better now.'

My saviour in a blue tabard nods me on my way.

Abandoning all hope of making myself more presentable, I step out of the station into the warmth of the evening sun, gait just a little bit unsteady. The clock at St Pancras says it's 6.15 p.m. Time to face Housmans and the past.

I leave behind the crowds around the station and turn onto Caledonian Road, dramatically quieter, with lots of old buildings and traditional businesses. I immediately spot a dark, stocky figure outside the unlit bookshop. Shivering despite the warm evening sun, I pull my sunglasses firmly down off my head to cover my red eyes, and adjust my scarf to cover the blotches on my neck and chest.

He turns as I approach. Raises his eyebrows. Then a giant bear hug. *Dan, Dan the union man*. He hasn't changed a bit.

'I'm so sorry.' He looks like he means it.

'Sorry? What are you sorry for?' I shake my head, extracting myself to look at his face.

'I brought this on you.'

So many years have slipped by because of that feeling, the unspoken guilt that's sat between us since Carlo left. Dan and I look at each other, locked in the moment, until a heavy hand on my shoulder breaches the wall of shame.

'A'right love?' *Liam. Scouse Liam.* Another bear hug. Time hurtles back.

'Liam!' I am genuinely delighted to see him in front of me again. Ten years. There is so much to say, and I don't know where to start. Somehow I land on: 'You know that I gave birth wearing that T-shirt you bought me? *No Guerra*? Remember, you brought it back from California?'

Liam looks both bemused and amused.

'She has twins, you know.' Dan clarifies things.

'Yes, it was a huge T-shirt!' Babbling, just nerves. *Breathe.*

Through this fog of nonsense, a short, muscular man in a flat cap appears. I vaguely recognise him from my Google searches.

'Donna, this is Dave Smith.'

'Hiya.' Firm handshake, no hug. Tough, I think.

'Who we waiting for now?' says Dan, getting edgy.

'Just Joe.'

'Let's wait in the pub,' I suggest, shivering.

After they scout the pub to see who looks suspicious, we squeeze around a small table at the back, as far from the rest of the clientele as possible. Liam checks his beeping phone. 'Joe can't make it, something's come up at work.'

'Is he still in homelessness?'

'Yeah, similar like, he's a community worker over in west London.'

'Switch your phone off.' Dan nods to me. I look at him quizzically but do as I'm told. I am no longer used to the rules.

Liam buys the first round, which is typical of him. A large white wine for me. 'Pinot Grigio all right for you?' he shouts from the bar. Pints of Moretti for them. Italian lager and Italian wine. How fitting.

'So . . .' I gulp from my glass too quickly, almost choking on the not-quite-cold-enough wine. Pause. 'So . . . what is it we're doing here?'

Dave looks at me like I'm an innocent abroad. Or possibly the village idiot.

'We're here to talk about Carlo.'

'Well, I gathered that. But what exactly are we doing? Tonight, I mean?'

Dan is more in tune with the state of my head. Of these three men sitting too closely round the table, he knows me best.

'We suspect that Carlo was an undercover cop, Donna.'

'Right.' Another huge gulp of wine. It has gone warm in my hands.

'Thing is, D,' Liam turns to face me, dark eyes burning in his steadfastly serious way, 'we've had suspicions about Carlo for a few years, but we started putting them together and it looks pretty much certain.'

Dave comes back in. 'We're working with a journalist called Rob Evans. You heard of him?'

'Yes. I've read the book.'

'You've read *Undercover*?'

'Yes.' Nodding, robotically. My jaw has stiffened up. 'My friend Tania brought it . . . you remember Tania, don't you?' I turn to Dan, seeking some familiarity, a connection amidst this strangeness. He nods yes. 'Well, she's moved back to Glasgow, but she came to stay a few weeks ago, and she had the book with her. She knew the undercover cop Peter Francis at the time, you see.'

The three of them look at me, aghast. They clearly weren't expecting this response. I tilt the glass to get the last drops. Christ, that's gone down quickly.

'Another one?' Liam gestures at my empty glass.

'No, it's my round, mate.' Dan is up on his feet. Liam has always been too generous. He would buy every round if you let him.

27

'So, you know the story?' Dave looks intently at me.

'I don't know what I know.' I shake my head. 'I just know that when I read the book the hairs stood up on the back of my neck, and everything seemed to click into place.'

'And that was it? You left it?' Dave twists his face into a grimace. I'm aware that my inaction sounds cowardly. I somehow have to explain myself to these men. They didn't avoid the truth about Carlo. I feel physical discomfort take hold again, waves of anxiety churning in my gut, and I notice my pulse is speeding up. My mouth is already dry, and I look longingly over at my drink as the barman pours it.

'I wrote an email. To you.' I look up at Dan as he puts my fresh wine glass on the table. I smile at him, nodding thanks. 'I wrote a long email. Then I deleted it.'

The three of them look awkwardly at each other. They have no idea what to say in response.

Dan starts to speak, then freezes. Dave steps in, measured and direct.

'Do you remember anything that made you suspicious at the time? Any particular events, strange coincidences, weird reactions that Carlo had?'

The question almost makes me laugh, a breath of irony caught in my throat. Now, every moment is steeped in suspicion, every glance and word lit differently. But I know that they are asking themselves the same question. They want to know how come we didn't all spot it.

I settle on a moment that was impossible to ignore, even then. 'He disappeared for a week. I was worried sick. He told me he'd been arrested in Italy, while he was there to see his dad, for peeing on a police car.'

'That takes the fuckin' piss!' Dave howls in his Essex accent.

'How come I didn't meet you when I was with Carlo?' I ask him, curious about his interest in my phantom relationship.

'I was married, had young kids. I wasn't out partying like you lot. I met Carlo through the trade union stuff. He was often seen on a picket line.'

'You're a rep?'

'Was. I'm a builder. Not on sites any more. I teach for the union now. Just about to start my PhD.'

'Ooh! Fancy! I looked you up and saw you've written a book. I must order a copy.'

'Don't be daft, here, you can have this one.'

Dave takes a copy of *Blacklisted* out of his messenger bag. His book is about the widespread blacklisting of construction workers, co-written with an investigative journalist called Phil Chamberlain.

I take the book from him, turning it over to read the blurb on the back. Blacklisted workers, hundreds of them, working collectively to expose the dark corruption of big business and the scandalous collusion of the state, both the police and the security services, in carrying out the shameful and immoral practice of blacklisting.

'It's like a modern-day *Boys from the Blackstuff*,' I say, 'but with added bent coppers.'

As I start to skim though the pages, I see now-familiar names. Harriet Wistrich, Helen Steel, Alison. Picking out moments, I see that Dave has woven some of the women's stories into the book and I realise how entwined their lives were with every part of the activist and trade union movements. In long days of internet research I've become involved with these women so intensely, I feel like I've known them for months. When I first read about them it felt like a parallel universe, a cast of characters and a situation that sat alongside my own life. The more I read, the more I recognised, the more I realised how interconnected we all are.

'God, Dave. I know lots of the people in your book. Is Carlo in here too?'

'No, we suspected he was an undercover cop, but hadn't found out enough when we were writing it. Your story will be in the next edition. If you want it to be, obviously.'

I don't say anything. I don't know what my story is yet.

Dave has to get back to Essex so says his goodbyes to us all. We exchange numbers and agree to keep in touch. In the strangeness of the moment, he feels like a grounding force, a solid man who knows how to manage this situation. I get the sense of a committed activist, a leader and a force for good, but a man who maintains a cheeky sense of humour. I could never be doing with all those overly earnest types you encountered on the left. The three of us who remain have consumed enough drops to relax into ourselves.

'Did you ask to meet his family?' Liam tilts his head to look at me, side on.

'Loads of times. Carlo kept saying we would go and visit his sister in Peterborough, but every time he'd say she was too depressed and didn't feel up to it. He would go on his own.'

'And his dad?'

'I wanted to visit him when we went to Bologna, as he lived in the countryside near Modena. Carlo said he just wanted us to have a romantic trip and seeing his father would ruin it. We stayed in a five-star hotel, ate out in beautiful restaurants. We even ordered breakfast in bed!'

I laughed at this ridiculous detail. It had been for his birthday and Valentine's Day. Now I could only be sure of the latter. Who knew if his birthdate was a fact or a fiction?

'So, what happened after you left Maida Vale?' Dan looks serious, concerned.

'I was slightly . . . broken after Carlo left. I was hounded out of the flat and I was assaulted on the Underground.'

They both look unbearably sad; guilty even.

'I was homeless – sofa-surfing, I suppose. I moved in with Steve; he let me have his box room for three months. If it hadn't been for him, I would have gone back to Scotland.'

'Steve?'

'Yeah, remember the manager of the mental health team? Gorgeous bloke. He left all this – homelessness and drugs work – runs a café in Brixton now. Vegan. Anyway,' I try to lighten the mood, having led the conversation down this dark alley, 'I went on the telly to talk about being homeless, the BBC *News at Six*. Then someone offered me a place on a game show. To win your own house.'

'You're joking?' Liam spits out his lager.

'No, it's all true, Liam! A game show for homeless people. The apparently interesting aspect of my story was that I myself was homeless, but I was also looking after homeless people.'

Dan shakes his head, utterly morose at the thought of this as entertainment. 'And Carlo? What did you think had happened to Carlo?'

'I heard from someone a year later that he'd gone back to Italy, got really fat and had an accident. Fell off his Ducati.'

We sit in a comfortable silence for a few moments. Like we haven't been estranged for ten years. There is an immediate reconnection. A patchwork quilt, our stories, knitting us all back together again.

'Right.' I stand up. 'My round this time. One for the road, then I better get myself back to normal life.'

*   *   *

Liam insists on walking me to the station. He's somewhat old-fashioned and I like it.

'Christ, I'm a bit wobbly.' I go over on my ankle, grabbing his elbow for balance.

'I'm not surprised, Donna. This must be a hell of a shock.'

'I don't know, Liam. I feel like I've known something – this secret. Like it's all been brewing for months now, churning away in my gut. Knowing it wasn't right. It was the book, I think, *Undercover*. The other women's stories really hit me.'

I look up at him as we stop, reaching the station entrance.

'I can't explain it, other than it feels like this thing happened to me too. It's fucking weird though. You live with someone for two years and then . . . they simply don't exist.'

'I can't imagine what it's like.'

'You knew him too though, or thought you did. It must have been a shock for you too?'

I want to share this feeling. I don't want it to be just me. We walk along side by side, shoulders almost touching. It feels safe.

'I thought we were mates. Never close. You know, D, even at the time there was something about him I wasn't sure about. Always thought you were better off without, to be honest.'

Perhaps now. But then, those months after he left – I never felt better off then, just desperately alone. I smile up at Liam anyway, wanting to reassure him for some reason.

'So what now?'

'Well, that's up to you, D. We're meeting a lot, working together to try to get to the bottom of it. I want him to face consequences, something to happen after what he did to us. To you. If you want to be part of that, I'll be there for you – we're in it together. But you can just walk away from it all if you want. None of us would blame you.'

The lights are pouring out of King's Cross station, and I turn to hug Liam goodbye without saying anything. Walk through the station without looking back.

I get on the train and put my bag beside me, not getting out my phone or my headphones. Instead, I look out of the window and simply watch London detangle and flatten out into countryside. My mind is blank, my brain just a mass pressing against the inside of my skull. My heart is pounding, and I tune in to the primal beat. *Feel something.* My truth is in my body at this moment. I slip off my boots, curling and uncurling my toes to get a sense of being alive. Nothing feels real any more. I catch my reflection in the train window. The wide, pale face looking back isn't me any more.

Perhaps it's the wine, or perhaps it's self-protection, but the journey home passes in a dissociated blur.

3

Uncovering the Truth

After that first meeting outside Housmans, I am drawn into a whole new world, engaging in a flurry of interactions with people I've never met before. Dave Smith is the architect, putting me in touch with all of them. I quickly realise how connected he is. He knows everyone. Journalists, politicians, activists from all the social justice movements. Trade unionists, environmentalists, animal rights activists, family justice campaigners. He is at the epicentre of the activist world. The new activist world, which is so different from the one I knew all those years ago. I spent my twenties and thirties with working-class socialists, a familiar and comfortable world. My father had been a full-time trade union convenor and I grew up with men being inflexibly, patriarchally men. The left had seemed static and grey. This new world feels much more fluid, with a colourful cast of characters.

I've barely drawn breath in the two weeks after that evening in the pub. When I'd got home from London I'd crawled into bed and just slept, all through the night and well into the next morning. I'd woken to several messages from the activists: polite, supportive, interested. I'd left them aside and gone out for a walk with the girls, kicking pebbles down the beach while they dragged at my hands, desperate to go home. But by the time we were eating lunch, the girls chatting away while I chipped in every so often, I knew I wasn't going to leave the message. I knew I couldn't let the truth slip through my fingers again.

I respond to a message from Dave and within an hour he has replied, inviting me to the next meeting. This one will be near Euston station. Liam will be there, Steve, Joe, Dan again, and a few others whose names I recognise from the past. So much is happening so quickly that I feel it is going over my head. I decide I should take notes from now on and write on my hand 'buy notebook'. For all that the details of the case pass over my head, the stories I've heard and read about the other women stay with me. The knowledge that I am becoming one of them.

Over coffees and pints between Kent and London I've spoken about what happened, dug into the story of my relationship for more people than I could keep track of. They say it's important to know everything, that as they build a case against the police they need every bit of evidence they can get, every hint of deception and sign of a piece in a bigger puzzle. Each person is careful, caring, but I know I'm one story, a puzzle piece. Many of them are pieces in the puzzle too, people who've been spied on by Carlo or another undercover cop. As they share stories too, I'm caught by the knowledge that Carlo had this entire life beyond us: friends, acquaintances – a whole world he'd built around his lie. Somehow, I'm able to go through it, relaying the key moments, revealing the main events. People have asked me about every detail. Except how I felt, then and now.

After two weeks, another man is sent my way with questions. Peter Salmon (an alias) gets in touch, at a prearranged time. I've realised that most roads lead back to Peter, a dedicated researcher at the heart of the investigation. He is a committed environmental activist and got involved in the immediate after-math of the Mark Kennedy story, meeting with other activists and women involved to try to put the network together. Famously rigorous, it was Salmon who pored over documents to try to find out what police were undercover, and who they really were. It was Dan, Steve and Dave who'd first suspected Carlo, but it was Peter who'd done the rigorous research and put him firmly on the map, who'd first found the evidence to confirm their suspicions.

I wait for the call in my upstairs office/study, snapshots spread out in front of me on the old desk I bought off eBay. Carlo and me at Whitby Abbey, Carlo by himself, lounging in a chair in the bar of a fancy hotel, grinning for the camera. Carlo with my mum, his hugeness dwarfing her. I've gone through boxes of papers, photos, everything. I could not find the cards he sent me. This is annoying me. Where have they gone? They appear to have vanished into thin air. I've kept everything. I even found a bundle of postcards and thank-you cards addressed to us both, thanking us for our hospitality and lovely dinners. To 'Tootsie and Rocco' from my sister. Carlo's nickname for her was Tallulah. So long ago, yet the images, the laughter, are so vivid.

I jump when the phone rings.

'Hello, is that Donna?'

Peter Salmon is softly spoken, with a gentle Irish lilt. He works for an organisation called the Undercover Research Group. The group is made of a small set of experienced activist-investigators who individually and collectively have already been researching state and corporate spying for many years. The majority of exposures of spycops/corporate spies in the mainstream media were prompted by the research of activists. In the case of Mark Kennedy, it was Lisa who discovered the truth. She discovered he had a passport in the unfamiliar name of Mark Kennedy. She knew him as Mark Stone. The worst thing was seeing that he had a child, added onto the passport. Stone did not have a child, but clearly Kennedy did.

Lisa also found a secret mobile phone that was rarely used and discovered emails from two children, calling Mark 'Dad'.

With help from her activist friends, she started to dig into his life. Eventually they found a birth certificate for Kennedy's son, which recorded Kennedy's occupation as being a police officer.

Lisa and her friends decided to confront Kennedy. One of the group asked him directly when he had joined the police. He confessed, and later cried.

The researchers work closely with investigative journalists, such as Rob Evans at the *Guardian*. The core group of three work across a larger network of committed activists, drawn from across the spectrum of progressive social justice campaigns.

Peter Salmon explains in his quiet, deliberate way that he wants a list of names, places, visits, events. This will help to fill in the gaps about Carlo. When did I live here and there, when did we visit so and so, what year did Carlo's dad die? When did he tell me about the child in Cornwall? What was my postcode in 2002? I remembered every detail.

'Did you keep a diary?' he asks.

'No, it's just clear in my head. There were so many specific events: birthdays, gigs, holidays. I can create a map around those. I've always had a good memory.'

'That's good news for us.'

He says goodbye after that, but not before saying he'll call again soon. I sit looking at my battered old phone on the table, my body completely still aside from a slight tremor in my hand. I feel like I'm living two lives, each disconnected from the other. The kids don't have a clue what's going on. I have a mental health group this evening. My energy levels are low, and I am easily distracted. I half-heartedly think about making lunch before I organise myself for the group. I have certificates to print off, as it's the last session of this cohort. I must buy cake on the way back from picking the kids up from school. The mood should be celebratory, but the phone call is still preoccupying me.

During one of the many phone calls that follow, this time to arrange a follow-up meeting in London with the wider group of activists that Carlo spied on, Dave asks if I have met any of the other women affected.

'No, I don't know any of them. I've heard of Helen Steel, obviously.'

'I'm not good with the emotional support,' he admits. 'You should meet Helen. I'll ask her to email you.'

The smartly dressed woman with short hair peers over her glasses at me.

'Donna?' She gestures for me to come and sit at the small table in the busy coffee shop.

'Yes . . . Alison?' How does she know it's me? We've only had an introduction by email, via Dave Smith. Alison is one of the original eight women to take a case against the Metropolitan Police, along with Helen Steel. I've arranged to meet the two of them in Patisserie Valerie at St Pancras station.

'Fucking paper cup! I pay this much for a coffee I want a proper cup! Hang on, just sit down, I'm going to change it. Do you want coffee?'

'Black, please.'

'I'll ask for it in a proper fucking cup!'

She returns with two cups of coffee in ceramic mugs. 'Helen's late as usual. Right. So, when did you actually find out? Hang on, first, do you know who I am?'

'Yes, I've read a bit. I read *Undercover*, last year, before I found out about this.' I am struggling to say his name. *Before I found out about Carlo*. 'Your story gave me the shivers. That's when something first clicked. That it wasn't right. The breakdown, how he left.'

Alison had lived with an undercover cop called Mark Jenner, who she knew as Mark Cassidy. He lived with her solidly for five years. Five years. I had a strong emotional reaction when I read her story. Something about the way he left the relationship. The breakdown. The way he changed.

'So, you were with Carlo for how long?' She's had a bit of a brief from Dave, but I can see her ferocious brain working overtime to put all the pieces in place.

'Just over two years. From September 2002 until November 2004.'

'And you lived together?

'Yes. We got engaged.'

'Fucking hell! Have you got any photos?'

I take out my phone and find the Dropbox folder marked 'CN', turning the screen around to show her the six photos I found and scanned into the computer. I had gone through old boxes and lever arch files, not sure what I would find. Digging up the past. I'm sure there are more pictures, somewhere.

'God, look at you. Don't you look lovely?' She lifts her head to peer at me. 'How old were you in this photo?'

'Thirty. It was my sister's graduation, so we were all dressed up.'

'He met your family?'

'Yes, lots of times. He loved them. Well, you know. It seemed like he loved them. We all went on holiday together.'

She nods, looking over her glasses again.

'Fuck, he's big, isn't he? Got big thighs. So did Mark. Did he like motorbikes by any chance?'

'Loved them. We had one. A Suzuki. His email address was "MinesADucati".'

'Bet he knows Jenner. Bastards, the pair of them.'

Helen Steel arrives ten minutes later, mouthing an apology. She's an icon of the activist movement and it feels odd to be sitting across the table from her. She looks just like her photos. Neat, dark hair with a serious fringe. I'd watched the *McLibel* film with Tania in her wee house in south London, before we both packed up and moved away. Helen was an environmental and animal rights activist, and a member of London Greenpeace. She had taken on McDonald's, representing herself in court, but with pro bono support from a young Keir Starmer. Franny Armstrong directed the documentary, which followed her battle against the corporate bullies, Helen holding the camera and the court throughout.

Helen was in a two-year relationship with an activist called John Barker. He disappeared from her life having apparently suffered a breakdown. She spent years searching for him, travelling across continents to try to find him, convinced he was in great distress. One day, when Helen had left after another day in court on the McLibel case, she passed St Catherine's House, which used to be the registry of births, deaths and marriages for England and Wales. Helen describes having a sudden instinct to go in and start looking through the death records for Barker. She was shocked to discover that her ex-partner had been using the name of a child who'd died at the age of eight.

John Barker disappeared in 1992 and Helen finally got confirmation that he was an undercover policeman in 2011, almost nineteen years later. His real name was John Dines. Helen discovered that the police actively took steps to prevent her and the other women from discovering the truth. They had an alert system in place so if someone looked up a particular birth or death certificate it would trigger an alarm and they would know you were looking for them. Helen was also told that when she went to New Zealand to search for John, they then moved him to another country to prevent her from finding him.

Alison and Helen were two of eight women who had recently won a historic case against the Metropolitan Police. This case was first launched in December 2011 against the Metropolitan Police and the Association of Chief Police Officers (ACPO). It consisted of eight women who were deceived into long-term intimate relationships by five officers who had infiltrated social and environmental justice campaigns. The women were represented by Birnberg Peirce & Partners. The women asserted that the actions of the undercover officers breached their human rights as protected by the European Convention on Human Rights, including Article 3 (no one shall be subjected to inhumane and degrading treatment) and Article 8 (respect for private and family life, including the right to form relationships without unjustified interference by the state). The women also brought claims for deceit, assault, misfeasance in public office and negligence by management.

The case included both common law claims and human rights claims. In both parts of the case the women faced legal challenges by the police, who repeatedly tried to strike out the case and have it sent to a secret court for reasons of national security, and who attempted to hide behind a blanket policy of Neither Confirm nor Deny.

The Metropolitan Police finally agreed that they had abused the women's human rights, in a comprehensive apology that was part of the settlement of the case. It had been a four-year legal battle, these women at the heart of a group pursuing the truth at any cost. The settlement was about to be made public, with a full televised apology and a press conference. The women had been deceived into relationships by police officers spying on activist groups, spanning a period of nearly three decades.

It had started with Mark Kennedy. Long-haired, covered in tattoos, a freelance climber and a true activist, known as Mark Stone to his friends in the environmental justice scene. He took part in almost every major environmental protest across Britain and Ireland from 2003, and infiltrated groups of anti-racists, anarchists and animal rights protesters. Using his fake passport in the name of Mark Stone, Kennedy visited over twenty countries, protesting against the building of a dam in Iceland, touring Spain with eco-activists, and infiltrating anarchist networks in Germany and Italy.

Kennedy was so well known in the activist community that two hundred people turned up for a three-day party for his fortieth birthday, shared with another activist.

He was focused more on the practicalities of demonstrations than the politics, and was fearless in the enacting of them. Kennedy chained himself to Hartlepool nuclear power station, climbed a crane at Didcot Power Station. His career concluded in an operation at Ratcliffe-on-Soar Power Station, a coal-fired plant owned by E.ON. In a £300,000 operation police swooped into a school building where protesters had gathered. Presumably tipped off by Kennedy, who was also inside, the police found over a hundred activists in the school. Twenty protesters were convicted of conspiracy to commit trespass after they admitted they had planned to occupy the plant for a week.

When Kennedy was unmasked by Lisa, the police claimed he was a rogue officer, admitting to undercover policing but distancing themselves from the man himself. From his ties to the activist community, and from his sexual relationships, with Lisa and a number of other women he was sent to spy on. Against the police 'code of conduct', apparently.

After Kennedy was exposed in 2010, and investigators started finding more names and details of undercover police, it was clear many of them had had long-term relationships with women in the groups they were spying on. These women began to meet up with each other. Together with campaigning lawyer Harriet Wistrich and investigative journalists, the group exposed their spycop ex-partners through a series of media reports. As the women began to provide their accounts and share their stories, it became clear that the behaviour of the men in the relationships, their backstories and exit strategies were markedly similar, suggesting systematic methods of infiltration. These patterns and signs completely undermined the myth of the 'rogue officer'.

In 2011, Tom Fowler, 'Deborah' and one other woman began a court action against the Metropolitan Police Force, South Wales Police Force and the Association of Chief Police Officers due to undercover cop Marco Jacobs' intrusion into their lives. Jacobs infiltrated political groups within the activist and anarchist movement between 2004 and 2009, in Brighton and Cardiff. Jacobs left Cardiff in 2009, telling his friends that he was moving abroad for work. Shortly after leaving, all communication from him stopped. In 2011, after some months of speculation among the activist community in Cardiff, Tom and the two women did their own investigations. The *Guardian* then reported that Marco Jacobs was an undercover police officer.

Despite having publicly apologised to the original eight women for such deceitful long-term intimate relationships and abuses, the police continued to enact their stalling tactics in the

South Wales case, trying to push back the timetable to trial as far as possible. The case was finally settled in 2017.

Helen and Alison had fought for years to expose the truth, alongside the other women who'd suffered deep trauma. Many of those women were still living under anonymity. At least two of the women had children with undercover police officers. They'd seen it all. Now, it seems, it's my turn to fight for the truth.

'I'm so sorry that this has happened to you.' I am surprised at how quietly spoken Helen is. It gives her a serious, measured air.

'How did you find out?'

I explain about Dan and Liam and Dave, and the message sent out of the blue.

'Fucking insensitive men.'

Until she said this it hadn't even crossed my mind. 'I'm meeting even more of them next week.'

'More of them?'

'Men. Not sure how insensitive these other ones are. That lot didn't seem too bad to me. Do either of you know Steve Hedley? Irish, from Derry? He's high up in the RMT union.'

'Hedders?!' Alison splutters out a mouthful of flat white. 'Course I know Hedders! I travelled to Belfast and Derry with him! I even stayed in his mother's house. Mark spied on him! Did Carlo spy on him too?'

Steve Hedley was the well-known assistant general secretary of the National Union of Rail, Maritime and Transport Workers (RMT trade union). Scourge of the right-wing press, who loved to take sneaky pictures of him on holiday wearing Cossack hats. I'd heard him mentioned by other friends, Dan and Tania, but met him for the first time on the anti-war demonstration where I met Carlo. Carlo met Steve through Dan and seemed to have befriended him. Steve loved boxing and football – subjects that could keep them talking for hours.

Carlo, Steve and I got on well and the three of us ended up spending a lot of time together. We would go to gigs together, sing along to Christy Moore and Dick Gaughan. Steve and I had a shared love of folk music and curry. Tayyab's in Aldgate was our favourite, and we'd go in a group, or just the three of us. Steve was happy talking music, but we'd range over everything, Carlo always laughing, prompting. I'd join in or sit back, revelling in the company.

Steve and I were also studying at the same time, him for a master's and me for a diploma in substance misuse studies. We would email each other supportive messages when we were struggling to finish our essays. He had a sharp mind, and shared it generously.

'Yes, Carlo was very close to Steve. Steve was there the day of the Stop the War march, with his kids. He had the absolute nerve to move in with Steve and the girls when he left me! I'm meeting him and a bloke called Peter Salmon, who is a researcher, plus my friend Dan and Dave Smith. They want to try to piece together bits of information from me. Dates and stuff. They're trying to find out his real name.'

'Jesus Christ.' Helen shakes her head. 'You couldn't make this stuff up. I'll come with you when you meet them. Peter Salmon's not his real name, you do know that?'

'Yes, I had guessed.'

We move from the Patisserie Valerie in St Pancras station to a nearby pub, the Rocket on Euston Road. I discover that both Helen and Alison have birthdays this weekend. We're celebrating. And I'm now part of the club. We talk about our families and lives, the things we love and the things we don't, and I almost forget why we've all come together. That is until one of them asks who my lawyer is. I tell them I don't have one, not yet anyway. It's on the to-do list.

'No, you must go with Harriet Wistrich, our lawyer. She's fearless. She won our case and she's the best feminist lawyer in the country. I'll email her and introduce you.' Alison lifts up her rucksack. 'I'm going to the bar. White wine? Shall I get a bottle between us? Watch my phone; it's charging just there.'

Lawyers. Civil action. Claims against the Metropolitan Police.

'Have you thought about anonymity?' Helen asks, looking at me intently. I'm starting to get used to it.

Anonymity. I'd never even thought about anonymity beyond ITV dramas, and suddenly it was part of my identity. I'd known from the first reading about the undercover police investigation that many of the women had chosen a different name. The press scrutiny, not to mention the attention of the groups who were on the police's side, made it a good idea. I hadn't really thought about it, until it was suggested that I choose another name. Another victim, another name.

'Yes, I am now called Andrea. Chose the name completely off the top of my head. Peter asked me to come up with a name for his report that he's working on. He also suggested a lawyer. It's all happened pretty quickly.'

'Why did you decide on anonymity? Why not just be yourself?'

'I haven't really decided about the long term. It's just breathing space, for now. Did you never have anonymity, Helen?'

'No, I did too, initially. But it didn't work. I was too well known because of *McLibel* and the McDonald's case. It was ridiculous to try to maintain it. Two of the other women don't have anonymity. It can be a hindrance.'

'What about you?' I direct this to Alison, who has anonymity.

'No bloody chance! Too much of an invasion of privacy. Kids, work, family. I find it much easier having it. It's a layer of protection. Anyway, you can always drop it later on if you decide to.'

I'm trying to keep up with this onslaught of information. None of the male activists needed anonymity, did they? All these men – Steve, Dave, Dan. They were all spied on, they're all part of the movement against the police, they were all activists. They all have their own names. Was it the risk of scandal for the women, the hint of salaciousness due to the sexual relationships? Attracting unwanted attention?

'Back to lawyers.' Helen wants to hammer this home. 'You must go with Harriet. She will really look after you. And then there's the public inquiry to think about. Will you join as a core participant?'

My head was spinning with all this information. I hadn't thought about that yet. I didn't realise it would be such a big undertaking. The Undercover Policing Inquiry was announced in 2015 by Theresa May when she was home secretary in response to the shocking revelations about the women activists being deceived into relationships and the corrupt policing involved in the Stephen Lawrence scandal. It came about as a result of the pressure of women like Helen and Alison, the Lawrence family and trade union activists such as the blacklisted builders.

The inquiry would start soon, and all the activists I was talking to were focused on it as an opportunity for truth, if not justice. I'd watched inquiries before – men, mostly, around a table, interrogating another man on a microphone. I knew they were meant to be non-adversarial. They were meant to be truth-seeking and would make recommendations for the future. In theory, this process should hold our institutions to account. The press, the government, the police. For the women and the other activists this was the apex of their years of work, a chance to put the police on the spot, if not quite in the dock.

The uncovering of Carlo, my own involvement, had all come too late in the day for the civil case the women had won against the police. But I was right in time for the inquiry apparently. I wasn't so sure that made me lucky. It was going to be big news.

'When I met up with the guys they told me they're thinking about doing a joint story with the *Guardian*. And possibly a film, for *Newsnight*. They want me to get involved. They said the TV piece wouldn't really work without me. The relationships are such a big story. I mean, I realise the other stories are huge too: blacklisting, miscarriages of justice, police collusion. Anyway, I've agreed to meet Rob Evans on Thursday. He's coming to Folkestone.'

Helen looks at me, her eyes widening and her fingers gripping her pen intensely. I feel naïve, like I've wandered into a world that's too big for me. These are real activists. I'm making it up as I go along. I've lived my life guided by my intuition, which I'm now discovering, thanks to Carlo and the Metropolitan Police, hasn't always served me well.

'Don't be pushed into anything you don't want to do. And speak to Harriet before you agree to any media stuff. Get her approval on any articles before they are published. We've all had experience of media stories going wrong. A couple of the women had horrendous experiences. One had the tabloids knocking on doors trying to track her down. One of us will come with you to any meetings or interviews.'

Jesus Christ, I think to myself. This is all starting to sound a bit full-on. My stomach gives a lurch. Scary.

'You don't need to worry about Rob though,' says Alison. 'He's an old friend. You can trust him.'

*   *   *

I make a plan to see Rob, inviting him to my hometown, wanting to feel safe, in control of the environment. After the meeting is fixed, I text Alison:

> Thanks for your help and advice. I'm meeting Rob. Looking forward to it.

I'm not sure I am looking forward to it, but I am grateful to Helen and Alison for caring.

She writes back immediately:

> Good – let me know how it goes. And here's Harriet Wistrich's email address. Get in touch with her – you won't regret it.

I open up my email straight away, scanning over the read messages from Dave, Dan, Peter, Alison, and one from my mum in the midst of it. I type Harriet's email into the contact bar and stare at the subject line for several seconds.

'Case' feels too vague, Carlo's name too personal. I settle on 'Undercover Police'. She probably gets hundreds of emails with that subject.

> Hi Harriet
> Alison gave me your email address. I'm one of the women and hoped you might be able to help me?
> Yours
> Donna

The 'Yours' feels so formal, but I don't know how to address a lawyer, what they expect.

I leave my computer and make a cup of green tea, walk around the garden, come back to the table. She's already replied, asking to have a telephone meeting the next day. Her tone is formal, professional. I arrange a time to chat, mid-afternoon, knowing the girls will still be in school. As I press send on my reply I hear them crashing through the door, back from school, shouting my name. *Mum!*

My initial phone meeting with Harriet is short and precise. It is a fact-finding mission. She asks if I have instructed any other lawyer and I say no, this is my first communication with anyone apart from the activists. I briefly explain the history of my relationship with Carlo and then fast-forward to the present, to explain why I am now suspicious about Carlo. I explain the involvement of Rob Evans and Peter Salmon, as well as naming the key activists involved. Harriet seems to know most of the protagonists already. This feels reassuring.

Harriet explains that if we have enough evidence my options are to launch a civil case against the police and to become involved in the newly formed public inquiry into undercover policing, as a 'core participant', which is basically a witness. If I would like to proceed, we will have to meet up at her office in Camden to sign some paperwork and I will need to provide a detailed witness statement.

After the phone call has ended, I lean back in my chair and let out a huge sigh. Relief? I don't know. I'm part of something now. I didn't plan this, but it's happening. The undercover policing scandal is becoming part of my life now.

I meet Harriet Wistrich for the first time in person at the Birnberg Peirce offices in Camden. The place is hectic – not what I was expecting. The waiting room is full of clients who look like they are in desperate need of help. I expected a calm, elegant space with plants and arty prints on the walls. This is more like the waiting room of a hostel. I ask where the toilet is and splash my face with water, reluctantly catching my reflection in the mirror. I look ill. Red-eyed and blotchy. I don't recognise myself.

Harriet appears, wearing a grey trouser suit and a big smile. She calls me into a meeting room off a busy corridor of offices, which are all piled high with lever arch files. Phones are ringing everywhere.

'It'll be cooler than my office,' she says. 'Tea or coffee?' I opt for water.

Harriet lays out the formalities of instructing her as my solicitor.

She explains how the civil proceedings work, goes through the different stages of a civil case and tells me about cost risk. She can see it is going over my head. 'I'll email you a dummies' guide,' she says. 'Kate Wilson put it together for the original case of the eight women. Have you met Kate?'

'Not yet, I've met Alison and Helen.'

'I'm sure you'll get to meet the others soon. They are a formidable bunch.'

'Yes, I'm beginning to realise that.'

She smiles again. 'Right, let's crack on.'

The witness statement is a taste of things to come. Detail after detail. When did Carlo and I meet? How quickly did we enter into a sexual relationship? How often did he stay with me?

'All the time,' I reply. 'He moved in pretty much immediately.'

She raises her eyebrows.

'We got engaged.'

'Engaged?'

'Yes, he proposed that Hogmanay, three months after we met.'

'Did he buy you a ring?'

'It never materialised.' I want the grey carpeted floor to open up and swallow me into the bowels of Camden. I feel so stupid.

The worst part is replaying the beginning of the end of the relationship. I tell Harriet, the famous feminist lawyer, all about Carlo's mental breakdown and his traumatic childhood, the history of sexual abuse and domestic abuse in his family.

Her brow furrows. 'So cynical, so manipulative. God, they are cruel.'

We arrange a follow-up phone call the next week and Harriet tells me her secretary will be in touch with a copy of the witness statement for me to check and sign.

On the train home I get messages from Helen and Alison to check how I am feeling. And an email from Harriet – reassurance, next steps. As London disappears, I feel like these women are coming with me.

4

Telling Tales

I apply my make-up in a shell-shaped compact mirror at the kitchen table. Black eyeliner, flicked up at the edges. A light dusting of coral blush. I can see some new lines appearing at the corners of my mouth. I'm curious about them, inspect them like a scientist would, but they don't particularly annoy me. Glancing at the clock, I see I have ten minutes to spare, just enough time to hang the washing out. The sun is shining in my small courtyard garden and the dogs are spread out under the washing line – the warmest patch. One of them jumps when I accidentally scrape the rusty clothes pole on the concrete slabs and it emits a high-pitched screech. Polo shirts, gym shorts, knee-high socks, swimsuits. Two of everything. I smile as I hang a rainbow T-shirt on the line.

The girls are at school, so I've got the space and time to prepare for the interview. Helen's words have stuck with me, and though she said I could trust Rob, I am wary nonetheless. The media was instrumental in exposing the story and investigating it. Every step of the way the women and the activists worked with Rob Evans to get to the truth. It was Rob Evans who broke the story on Peter Francis, the police whistle-blower; it was Rob that the activists called when they discovered Mark Kennedy wasn't who he said he was. It was Rob who had helped activists to expose the other men, who'd made it possible to tie it back to the police at the highest level. Who'd given it the public attention so they couldn't back away.

When you work in homelessness and addiction, you know something else about the media though. I'd seen vulnerable people painted as some sort of scourge enough times to know the paper could take sides and it might not be yours. Women valiantly fighting for the truth, that's a good story. But it's not the only story the papers might want to tell. Especially as most of them are tied in as closely with the establishment as the police, the politicians.

The women involved in this story, the victims of the 'spycops', they were gold dust to the press. And they were essential to getting the story out there too. Helen was right to warn me. I was right to be wary. Rob Evans felt like a different case though, and everyone involved had told me he was on our side, rigorous, dedicated, fair, supportive. He'd spent his career investigating some of the most awful abuses of power in the country, scrutinising the inner workings of government across surveillance and other complex issues.

I wear boots, a thick jacket pulled around me. I lock the house and find myself going back to check it after going a few steps.

I've agreed to meet Rob Evans outside Central train station and I recognise him instantly.

'You look just like your photo,' I say, my hand outstretched.

He shakes my hand. He has a funny little giggle and good skin.

'Are you happy to walk into town? It's a lovely day.'

He seems reluctant. 'Is it far?'

Typical Londoner, I think. 'Less than ten minutes' walk. Or we can jump in a taxi.'

'Fine, let's walk.'

I steer him towards the pedestrian crossing, where a learner driver comes to a shuddering halt as we step out. We chat about driving lessons on the way. I still haven't passed my test and only recently abandoned manual lessons for automatic, as I thought it might be easier. My driving instructor suggested it, fearful for his clutch.

'Moving to the seaside and getting two dogs is insane when you don't drive. Some of the buses here only run once an hour.'

'I had to learn,' he replies. 'Hated it, absolutely hated it, but had no choice.'

Rob had moved to the countryside and now commutes into London three days a week, working on investigative stories for the *Guardian*, as well as writing his books.

The café I've chosen is deserted, tables of all shapes and sizes spread over three floors, with mirrors and extravagant light fittings and lots of nooks and crannies. It doubles as an antique shop and everything is for sale.

'Let's sit here.'

I choose a shady corner table, partially obscured by a large potted fern. It occurs to me that while, being a relative newcomer, I don't know that many people in the town, it would be sod's law for a familiar face to show up here today.

We order coffees and then we set about excavating my past.

'If it's okay we'll start right at the beginning. I know some of this already from Dave and Peter, but it will be good to get it all down, in the right order, from you.'

Rob has a proper journalist's notebook, lined, and a cheap biro at the ready. I had expected a fancy pen.

'So, when did you first meet Carlo?'

I am instantly transported back. That day was bathed in acid colours, a Lichtenstein painting. Carlo was wearing a yellow high-vis vest over a sky-blue T-shirt with a nondescript logo, polarised sunglasses masking his eyes. They looked expensive. I had twisted my shiny chestnut hair into loose bunches, and an amber bindi winked out from my forehead. My belly proudly displayed its new tattoo, a self-designed mosaic of red and purple hearts. I had recently lost two stone, due to the relationship breakdown and its aftermath. But I looked fit and healthy, like I'd been on a spa break.

We had met among half a million people, marching through London on 28 September 2002. It was the biggest political demonstration Britain had seen in thirty years. Simultaneous protests happened around the country, on a scale not seen since 1968. We were there to voice our disgust at the impending invasion of Iraq. We knew that Tony Blair was wrong in supporting the US and George Bush. We didn't believe the speculation about weapons of mass destruction. What we foresaw was an illegal war and the murder of hundreds of thousands of innocent human beings.

So many people I knew were at that march, pulled in from different parts of London. I'd spent the morning texting people and getting myself ready, then I'd travelled down on the Bakerloo line alone, planning to meet my trade union comrades in the midst of the crowds at the Embankment. It was heaving from Tottenham Court Road down, groups of people chanting and singing. I'd joined the rush, working my way around the edges to the main surge, where I hoped I would find the Unison banner.

I had first noticed Carlo on Piccadilly, leaning against the railings of St James's Park, on the edge of the slow-moving crowd. I spotted Dan, a trade union activist, first, visible in his neon steward's vest. I waved frantically and then headed towards him, ducking my head under the sea of red trade union banners and Palestinian flags. I was relieved to see a familiar face. I snaked around the outside of the crowd, avoiding being trampled on by the army of black Palladium boots. Carlo was standing behind Dan, his manner casual yet commanding. Dan was stocky, but Carlo was the size of a bull. I sensed that he was watching my movements from behind the secretive shades.

Dan introduced him, the dark stranger. Carlo hadn't said a word.

'Donna, this is Carlo. He's a comrade from Bologna, came back to London a year ago.'

Carlo nodded at me, casual. I couldn't take my eyes off him.

I smile at the memory, forgetting the journalist in front of me. Rob looks at me quizzically, so I pull myself back to the present and start recounting the facts. I leave the emotion, the impact and the deep love for Carlo out of it. *Focus on the facts.* When I get to our romantic trip to Bologna, a present for Valentine's Day and Carlo's supposed thirty-second birthday, Rob's eyebrows rise; he's clearly interested. It was a visit to see the memorial plaque at Bologna Centrale train station, where the fascists had planted a bomb in 1980, killing eighty-five people and wounding over two hundred.

Rob looks up from his notebook. 'Really? He took you there?'

'Oh yes. It felt like a pilgrimage.'

'Was that the main event of the trip? Did you visit family, go further afield?'

I hesitated. 'No, no. Just us. Carlo didn't want to see his father.'

'And you weren't suspicious about not meeting his father while you were in Italy?'

'I understood the difficulty of coming from a fractured family.' I look him straight in the eye. 'I've had similar experiences.' *A jolt. Is it wise to be so candid with a journalist?*

He nods and returns to his scribbling.

*   *   *

I finally get around to the day that Carlo moved his things out. He had chosen to do it while I was at work, turning up in his estate car to clear the flat of his belongings. I try explaining to Rob the emptiness of it, how Carlo had taken everything with him, every book, cup, saucer that he had brought, right down to the last teaspoon. It felt like a forensic operation.

I'd been at work, sitting at my desk working my way through various small, easy tasks. I knew it was coming; he was staying with Steve already then, and we'd not spoken much for a couple of weeks. But each evening I'd come home to our flat, our things. Put on an album we shared, cooked in the pan he'd bought, watched TV. Alone but I'd pretend to myself that he was just out. He texted he was 'going round today' and I hadn't replied, not knowing what to say. The rest of a day was a blur, the evening spent in tears.

Rob is watching me, pen loose in his hand as he listens. His face is a picture of sympathy and I wonder if it's a look they're trained in or his genuine response. After a few hours with him I suspect it's the latter.

I suddenly spot a couple I know being seated by the waitress two tables away. *Damn*. The place is empty. Why sit them right beside us? I shoot Rob a look of warning, a slight nod to the side, indicating that we need to watch what we say now.

'Hiya!' I shout over. They're parents I know from the school gate.

They wave back cheerily. 'Hi, Donna, how are you?'

'Yes, good, thanks. You?' I smile at them and then nod to Rob, who is writing away again.

'Work meeting. We're just doing some planning. Mental health.' I don't think they will recognise him from the *Guardian*.

∗   ∗   ∗

Rob pays the bill. I can't focus on telling my story with the school mum and dad sitting so close by.

Standing outside the café, I realise I'm ravenous. I've had two strong black coffees and nothing to eat in the two hours since we met.

'What train do you want to get back to London?'

Rob checks his watch. 'Preferably getting into London no later than four?'

'All right, we have an hour. Do you fancy a bag of chips, since you're at the seaside? The promenade is just there, it's called the Leas, where the Victorians would meander up and down. It's just behind that row of shops. We can find a bench to sit on and I can finish telling you the story.'

'That's ambitious! It's a big story.' He laughs and we cross the road to Papa's, which is advertising a special cod and chips for £1.99.

'Bloody hell, that's cheap,' he says, holding the door open for me.

'I'm paying for the chips!' I laugh. 'Loads of vinegar, please,' I say to the woman behind the counter shovelling a mountain of chips into the tray. 'And a Diet Coke too.'

Too much caffeine today, I think. I'll be losing the run of myself.

We head back into the street and cross the main road, skirting down a side street to the beach. We find an empty wooden bench, dedicated to a deceased local. It looks directly out to sea. You can just make out France, and the shadow of Dungeness power station. We are sharing a large portion of chips, which would easily feed a family of four. Freshly cooked and not too greasy, the chips are wrapped in the local *Herald*, a delightful rag that carries a front-page story about supposed benefits scroungers.

'So how did you find his real name? I couldn't quite work that out from Peter's notes,' Rob asks, munching away at the very vinegary chips. I realise I didn't ask if he minded me having them doused so heavily in malt vinegar.

At the point when the activists approached me, Dave, Steve and Peter Salmon, they knew Carlo was a cop, but they didn't know his real surname. One could guess that Carlo was really his first name, as that was the pattern so far. But the surname had eluded them. I think part of their reason for approaching me at that point was to enlist my help in putting the final bit of the jigsaw into place.

Not only did I want to know what his real name was, it began to obsess me. It kept me awake at night. I wanted to know who he really was. I'd wanted to know who he was in real life. What books did he read? Was it Primo Levi and Robert Tressell? Or did he read pulp crime fiction? What did he watch on TV? Arthouse documentaries or *Top Gear*? I suspected it was *Top Gear*.

But of course, there was a bigger point. Knowing his true identity was vital to making the case. The more of the truth we could find out about Carlo, the bigger our case against the Met, and the more detail for the inquiry. We would want to know what he did next, after his undercover operation was over. Did he go on to manage other officers? Did he train them in the ways of deception?

Those early conversations, in the week after I first met Dave, they'd wanted to know every detail. I'd gone through every moment again and again, not entirely sure why I was repeating myself. But this was why: it wasn't just to uncover what happened to me, it was to find clues as to who Carlo was. They'd taken every thing I'd said and combined it with everything they knew to create a network of hints at Carlo's true identity. I'd imagined a big whiteboard with lots of photos and string linking names, like something in a police procedural. And a file full of discoveries, fodder for the inquiry. I was still processing everything I'd learned about the man I'd loved.

I take a gulp of my fizzy drink and then begin where I left off.

'Well, thanks to Peter Salmon and the other researchers, we had the name of the Italian import/export company, and we knew from Companies House that Carlo was named as a director. That was a moment of huge clarity for me. All that fancy food and wine we had in abundance obviously come from the food company!' I laugh, shaking my head. 'We really were living like champagne socialists then. We used to get taxis to demos, had people round for dinner all the time. Carlo always did the cooking. We had a meal out at least once a week and we even stayed in a five-star hotel in Bologna. Mind you, I had a good job at the time. I paid for that, as a treat for Carlo's birthday. Well, his fake birthday.'

Rob looks up from his scribbling. 'Such well-paid liars. Do you know how much they earned, and the expenses they had access to? They were on eighty grand a year, ten years ago. Public money. It's astonishing.'

'Bloody hell. What a world of madness.'

'And the family deli, what do you know about that?'

The family deli. A small Italian place on a leafy street. Peter and the team had been rooting out any connection they could find to Carlo, showing me leads to get my take. It felt like I'd been digging through the lives of every Italian in London. I'd read the girls a story, have a glass of wine, then look at endless documents.

'Well, it solved the puzzle, didn't it? I recognised Carlo's sister on the deli's Facebook page, from the picture of her on my bookcase. He brought real photos of his real family into our life. Sick, isn't it?'

Rob nodded sympathetically. 'How did you find out about the deli in the first place?'

'Carlo was also registered as a company director.'

'Fuck!' Rob is shaking his head, incredulous. 'So he tripped himself up?'

'Once you uncover one clue you just keep finding more . . . I must tell you the story of good cop/bad cop Carlo.'

Rob laughs. 'What's that about?'

'There is another Met cop called Carlo that the researchers came across via a newspaper search and they initially thought he might be THE Carlo. Anyway, my lawyer Harriet was talking to her partner and it turns out she knew that cop called Carlo. I had to email her a photo to confirm that it wasn't him. She was so relieved. She'd worked with good Carlo, helping women who were trafficked to safety. Mine was obviously the bad Carlo. Don't think women's safety was quite his thing.'

My mind blurs, goes strangely blank. It's done that recently, zapping in and out of reality. Some days, some moments, I still cannot fathom that this has happened. To me. My eyes focus on Rob, pen poised, looking at me quizzically.

'Sorry, Rob, I zoned out there. Where had I got to?'

'The deli.'

'Of course. So, through his research, Peter Salmon found out there was a deli/restaurant connected to the family's Italian food import/export business. The same names came up as directors. Peter had been contacted by my friend Dan and Dave Smith, after the activists had all got together to discuss their suspicions about Carlo.'

'Yes, I was there. They all came to meet me. This was before Peter and the other researchers who are part of the Undercover Research Group got involved. They didn't come in until after 2013.'

I inhaled sharply. 'You were there when they first met up? I hadn't realised.'

'Yes,' he said, without concern. 'It was around 2012. Dave and Phil Chamberlain contacted me, as they had started writing their book on blacklisting. Then the whole gang came to meet me at the *Guardian* offices. Dan, Dave, Joe, Steve Hedley. I remember it was a sunny day and we all went for a drink by the Regent's Canal. They talked about the suspicions they had about Carlo and the way he disappeared. Then Mark Kennedy was unmasked by his partner and the other women started to join forces. Peter Francis had also come forward and blown the whistle, so to speak. They realised there was a pattern and Carlo fitted it.'

'Oh my God. I was oblivious to this. No one thought to tell me until now? Three years later?!' I'm stunned. How could they know for so long and not try to contact me? I thought they had only just worked it out.

Rob shakes his head at this.

'Anyway, back to my story. Don't write that last bit down. I'll be having words with that lot myself.' I compose myself, breathing deeply, trying to drop my irritation. *Three years*. 'So by now it was established that Carlo's dad and his sister, *and* her husband, were all directors of the company. I realised then that his father hadn't died of a stroke on New Year's Day, 2004. He was still very much alive and well, living in London, in 2011. Lying shits. Do you know I bought vitamins for Carlo to take to Italy for him, when he supposedly had a stroke?'

I stare down morosely at the remaining chips, now cold and lifeless. At odd times it just hits me. Makes normal life stop dead. Work, kids, the everyday stuff becomes suspended out of my reach, as if someone has built an invisible wall between us. A horrible, dense wall that no one else can see, but which separates me from my own reality. I'm beginning to realise the extent of this massive deception. I'm playing catch-up with my own life and it feels like my own sense of stability, my very being, has been twisted and violently shaken by a sinister external force.

'Secrets and lies, Rob. It's mind-blowing that the British state could do this.'

5

Family Ties

In the weeks after my meeting with Rob, I realise I'm exhausted. This phenomenon of telling your story, time and time again, takes it out of you. I notice a physical tension; my neck, jaw and shoulders feel stuck, and I know I'm grinding my teeth at night. I decide to have some acupuncture, to try to find some sense of equilibrium. I find a local clinic in a town not far along the coast, a small, calm room. As I lie down, my bare back exposed, I can feel the tension under my skin. The acupuncturist doesn't say much, just slowly works her way down my body, inserting small needles. I'm not sure it does anything, but the hour lying still feels like a miracle.

The day-to-day demands of my life haven't changed. Mental health groups, kids, dogs. Every morning, a routine broken by the chatter of those around me. I haven't told the girls anything, but they climb into bed with me most mornings, suddenly needing to be close to me. I leave each group without a single memory of what happened in it, who said what. I don't think anyone notices, and the rest of the group say enough that my quietness can pass under the radar. But I'm easily distracted. When I try to focus on one task my mind jumps over three more.

Every evening I prepare dinner, put the girls to bed, then answer emails from the group. Sometimes I don't open my computer, I just watch crime dramas on TV until I'm exhausted enough to get into bed. I feel so far away from my friends and family. I'm starting to regret moving so far away from home.

Rob and I agreed to keep in touch about the article. He explained that it wouldn't be published for a while, possibly three months, as it will tie in with the BBC film. I'm not fully committed to this yet but have agreed for the *Newsnight* journalist to have my details, via Rob. A splash, he says.

My life is becoming a story. I feel like I'm acting out my life on stage, yet simultaneously I'm in the audience looking up at myself. It has all happened so quickly. So much information to take on board, legal jargon, working out who is important in the bigger picture, being sensitive to other people's stories. My thoughts are becoming jumbled, my normally sharp memory is dulled. I must write things down or I'll forget them. Even writing them down, though, I forget easily. I walk into a room and forget what it is I'm there for. This is a distant version of me, where sounds are muffled as if under water and faces become a blur. I don't like these sensations one bit.

My mum and my sister are due to come and stay, a last bit of sunshine before the end of summer. Unlike me, they are sun-lovers. I'm looking forward to seeing them, hoping they will bring some steadiness and normality back to my life. I'm increasingly homesick, wishing I could magic away all obstacles and get home to what is safe, what is known.

'Have you told your family yet?' Alison had asked me, in that grimy pub on the Euston Road.

'Not yet. They're due to visit at the beginning of next month. I'd rather tell them in person. I've no idea how my mum will react. My sister is going to be furious.'

'They will feel like their privacy has been completely invaded. From what you've said, they were very close to him.'

'Yes, they loved him. I'm actually dreading having to tell them. After The Artist left me, my mum and my sister swooped in and rescued me. I couldn't eat properly or sleep. I lived on those little French cheese triangles, Happy Cow, mixed in a bowl with chopped-up cherry tomatoes, washed down with aloe vera juice. Couldn't stomach eating bread. I was a mess.'

Alison screws up her nose at my makeshift crisis diet. I don't think she could ever be that feral, whatever state her life was in. I tell her about the day The Artist left me, having admitted to an affair with an actress he had known for a measly six weeks.

'Six weeks! I actually *begged* him to stay. Can you believe it?' I shudder at the thought of begging any man to stay. Never again.

'I remember an envelope from Scotland being delivered by the postwoman. She handed it to me, standing on the doorstep in a daze, as he was escaping with his hurriedly stuffed holdall. It had been my gran's ninetieth birthday party the week before and I had gone up to Scotland on my own, as he was far too busy painting a series of gargantuan heads. Too busy riding Miss RADA more like.'

Someone at the party had snapped a photo of my family on my mum's camera and she had sent me a copy. My gran, me, my sister, my mum and uncle. All beaming big smiles except me; my mouth was shut and my sharply bobbed dark hair was hiding my pale face. I looked odd, out of proportion, like I'd had something done to my lips. My gran was wearing a baby-blue cardigan, her favourite colour, leaning over her Zimmer frame to blow out the candles. The cake was big enough for all fifty party guests, a fruit cake covered in thick white icing and decorated with a leprechaun in a big hat who pointed at a sign saying, 'Happy 90th Birthday, Bridget!'

My legs had collapsed underneath me as his departure started to sink in, and I'd sat slumped in the hallway, looking at the outline of The Artist's latest giant portrait of his brother. Six massive canvases punctuated the dark hallway. I'd had enough of these blue-tinged faces leering at me, rictus-like. I wanted to be somewhere else, in a room with gentle landscapes; a cosy room with cushions and candles and a bit of love in it. When my mum arrived from Scotland to take care of me after the break-up she suggested, somewhat menacingly, that I take a Stanley knife to the paintings, but I could not bring myself to disrupt the art, regardless of what The Artist had done. They had a meaning of their own, beyond him.

I tell Alison the story of how I saved the portrait of The Artist's brother and how it went on to be accepted for the prestigious BP Award exhibition at the National Portrait Gallery.

'I had had the foresight to retrieve it from a skip near London Bridge. Heavy as fuck, it was. We had travelled from Maida Vale in a black cab, at great expense, to get it framed, but the framing shop was closed when we got there. The silly bugger hadn't phoned to check if they were even open on Saturdays. He lost his temper and threw his brother's massive head in the bin. I climbed into the skip and saved it while he raged off, all red-haired and red-eyed. He later calmed down, we got it framed in Tooting and he entered it into the competition. It was accepted. I could hardly take a Stanley knife to it after all that, regardless of what my mum said.'

'Good luck with it. Phone any time you want a chat.'

Truth is, I was so preoccupied I had barely registered the days passing until their visit was just around the corner.

'Oh my God, would you look at the size of you two!' My mum's first words. The same ones she says every visit. The kids have come with me to meet my mum and sister off the London train. Twins, but a four-inch height difference between them. One curly- and one straight-haired. They make my heart swell, looking at them cuddling my mum and my sister, then struggling to take their gran's big suitcase down the ramp in the station.

'Is there anything in there for me, Gran?' asks the curly one.

'Just a few wee things, darlin'.'

We all laugh. The blue suitcase with the floral ribbon is bursting at the seams.

It's a short walk from the station to my house. We pass the pub on the corner and the park, arriving at the house to hear the excited spaniel tails bashing against the front door.

'Can we get in, please?' The two dogs are wedged against the door, tails drumming excitedly at the arrival of guests. I huff at them as I lift my mum's heavy suitcase over the step, shooing the dogs away. A shoe and a wellington boot are wedged behind the door, gifts they've deposited.

'What have you got in here, Mum, house bricks?'

'Gran . . . Gran!! What have you got in your suitcase? Is it for us?'

'Give me a wee minute, girls.'

'Come on, I'll take the case into the living room so you can open it up.'

Once we've wheeled the heavy case into the living room, she unpacks the other, smaller bag in front of us, as the girls rebound off the walls and jump on and off the sofa. I realise I haven't seen them excited before, acting so much like little girls. They're getting older.

Gifts from Gran are duly dispensed: a bucketload of things for the kids, two of each thing, different but equal. Twins. Always fair. A cuddly Highland cow, a very woolly sheep, Burns for

Bairns, hooded tops in different colours and two boxes of Edinburgh rock. There's an excited opening of shiny things, packaging torn off and hugs given. My mum catches my eye as I lean against the wall watching the girls playing. Raises an eyebrow.

'Shall we have a cup of tea?' she says, an arm around each girl.

We all sit around the kitchen table. I'd moved it with me three times since picking it up in Camberwell. It had been abandoned by a previous tenant of the last sublet I had lived in. The table was hastily tidied up this morning, my piles of papers and books shoved in a corner, a precarious tower representing my life. A fresh bunch of yellow roses is now positioned in the centre of the table, an attempt to brighten up the room, which doesn't get much sun. I spot a huge cobweb looping from the ceiling to the window and wonder how long it will be before my mum comments.

'Wine?' I ask, glancing at the clock on the oven. It's half past five, almost not too early.

'Oh, why not, pet? We're on our holidays!' My mum loves her holidays, preferably somewhere hot and buzzy.

'We had a miniature bottle of prosecco each on the train.' My sister is relaxing now, on a much-needed break from her stressful job. 'And snacks.' She unpacks a bag and hands out more goodies.

'Girls – will you both take your presents from Auntie Laura next door, please? And play for half an hour?'

'But why, Mummy?' Fresh faces half look up at me, while half engrossed in their new trinkets.

'I want to talk to your gran and Laura about something, sweetheart.'

'What is it, Mummy?'

'Oh, don't worry, it's just something to do with Mummy's work. It would be boring for you two.'

My sister raises a quizzical eyebrow but says nothing. She is skilled in maximising her facial expressions. Off the girls go to the living room, small arms laden with neon pens and colouring books, animal hair clips and funky T-shirts.

'So, what's up?' she says, lifting her glass and taking a sip of Pinot Gris. I've bought fancier wine than usual, for them. Made a special trip to Waitrose.

I close the kitchen door, shushing the dogs from the hallway into their tartan bed in the corner. They are twins too, and they follow me everywhere.

'Well, I need to talk to you about Carlo.'

'Carlo?' my mum splutters, a fine spray of wine projecting onto the table, which she hurriedly wipes away. This is not what either of them had expected.

'Yes, Carlo.'

'Has he been back in touch with you? Tell him to get to—'

'No. No, Mum, he hasn't been in touch. Not directly anyway.'

I turn to my sister. 'Do you remember Dennis? And Dan?'

She nods, looking a bit worried. Of course she remembers. She knows them all well, having been to numerous dinners and parties with us in London, back in the early 2000s. What is coming next?

'Well,' I continue, 'Dennis got in touch with me a few weeks ago. He lives here in Kent now. We were friends on Facebook, but I've not seen him since 2005. Anyway, he asked if I would meet up to talk about Carlo. With Dan and Liam, and a trade union activist called Dave Smith.'

My sister looks serious but waits patiently for me to tell my story. My mum is desperate to jump in but restrains herself.

'So, I went to meet them in London—'

'What's he done?' My mum gives in to her curiosity.

'Well. It's kind of a long story. Have you heard in the news about the women who had relationships with men who turned out to be undercover police officers?'

'Yes,' says my sister. 'I've read about it. That guy with the funny eye. He was in Scotland for the G8. What's his name?'

'Kennedy. Mark Kennedy.'

'Yes, I remember reading about him. He was targeting environmental groups, right?' My sister has always been politically aware. It's one of the things we have in common.

'Well . . . Carlo was one of them too. He was really an undercover cop.'

I pause for a minute, looking at them both with an unusual seriousness. I want to let it sink in. Our biannual visits are normally jovial affairs. I wish I could have avoided this revelation for longer.

'Sorry, Mum, there's no easy way to say it. The Carlo you knew was not a real person. He was a fiction.'

'What?!' My mum is ready to explode. Her face is red, from the wine and incredulity. 'What do you mean? What are you saying, Donna?'

'What I'm saying is that we know for a fact that Carlo was not a locksmith. He was an undercover cop, working for Special Branch. He was sent by the state to spy on my friends.'

'But what had you done? Why you? I don't understand.'

'I hadn't done anything. And I know it doesn't make an ounce of sense, but I think I was a cover for him. At least I believe that's the case. I don't even have a criminal record.'

My sister shakes her head. 'God almighty.'

74

'Two years . . .' My mum taps her long nails on the table in a slow beat. 'You lived with him for two bloody years.'

'I know, Mum.'

'So, what was he actually doing?' My sister starts to nod her head, piecing the bits of this bizarre story together. 'Was he spying on Steve Hedley? Yes? Dan too?'

I nodded. 'I think so. I was with them both the day I met him. I think he was spying on Dan and Steve, and the others.'

My sister stares at her glass, a faraway look in her eyes. 'Now I think of it, he drove like a cop. Do you remember? The way he would weave in and out. He drove fast too. I've been in police cars with work.'

I shake my head. No, it has never crossed my mind that he drove like a cop.

'This book,' I say, to both of them. 'Please read this book.'

I hand my sister a copy and then offer one to my mum. I have two: one I was given by my friend Tania and one that Rob Evans gave me when we met.

'*Undercover*, by a journalist called Rob Evans. It will tell you everything you need to know.'

I pour another glass of wine, tipping the bottle up to get the last drops. We sit together in a rare familial silence, the pair of them flicking through their books, not really taking in any words.

March 2003. We were all together in Whitby for my thirty-first birthday. A cosy family get-together, organised after my mum fell in love with Carlo on our previous visits to Scotland and hers to London. She'd stayed for two days, during which he'd taken her out, made her Italian food and lavished her with attention. This trip was my mum, sister, stepdad and my sister's friend, who was engaged to a cop. They'd been together a few years, and at first we'd all been sceptical. She'd bring him along to birthdays, the pub occasionally. I was going home a few times a year in those days, getting the train up by myself and spending a few days at my mum's, sleeping on the couch at my sister's if we went out.

Carlo and I had spent half our relationship either at meetings or at marches, talking about the state and the 'powers that be'. I knew what Carlo thought of the police. He pulled a face when I warned him on the journey up not to say anything impolite about them, but he managed to behave himself in her company.

The family drove down from Scotland; Carlo and I travelled up from London. It was a long drive, wet and foggy as we wound our way up the east coast. He sang along to the CDs I chose – Marvin Gaye, Dusty Springfield, Elvis – and glanced at me, occasionally taking his eyes off the road, his hand rarely leaving its grip on my right knee. We arrived late on the Thursday evening, the night before my birthday, pulling up to the holiday flat at the end of a long, narrow road. It was Carlo who'd driven, Carlo who unpacked the bags and stood towering in the doorframe saying the first hello. We were ceremoniously shown to the master bedroom, its huge bed overlooking the harbour. My mum, on good form, cheeks flushed by a 'wee' Bacardi, insisted we take it. She cuddled Carlo, dwarfed by his size, stroking his arm in delight as he was wearing the floral shirt she'd bought him for Christmas. A generous bay window framed the sparkling night. Nautical prints in shades of blue on the walls.

'Look, isn't this room beautiful?'

'You should have taken it, Mum!'

A heavy mirror was propped against the wall on top of the chest of drawers, capturing the king-sized bed. The sight of that an invitation to him. Mischief glinting in his eyes.

'I'll leave you two to settle in,' my mum said, blushing. Happy.

In the pub later that evening, Carlo gave my mum his soulful eyes and told her that he was desperate for me to have a baby. We'd been together just six months.

I pulled back when he said it, looking at him, brow furrowed He was looking right into my mum's eyes though.

She turned to me, gleeful. 'Do you remember that fortune teller we went to in Ardrossan, Donna? She said you would have a baby with a dark-skinned man. You must have been sixteen then. We thought it would be with Jas, but no, it's with Carlo!'

I looked at Carlo, flushing with embarrassment. He patted my knee under the table.

My mum took another sip of Bacardi, giggling to herself. 'I can't wait to be a granny.'

My sister rolled her eyes, and I jumped in with a question to her friend.

We spent the rest of the evening eating, drinking, chatting and playing tunes in the living room overlooking the harbour. Carlo had brought two boxes of fancy wines and he acted as the waiter, keeping everyone topped up, when he wasn't keeping my mum amused. My mum and stepdad took themselves off to bed eventually, and we sat up finishing the wine with my sister and her friend. They'd shoot me thumbs-ups when Carlo wasn't looking, throwing wide eyes and smiles of encouragement my way. At last, it was the two of us, dancing arm in arm as he whispered in my ear. We didn't sleep that night.

The next day my sister took a snapshot of us in front of the ruins of Whitby Abbey, leaning in together and smiling in mirror image. My hair had sun-streaks and was swept over my face by the breeze, and Carlo and I were both wearing designer sunglasses. His were black and mine were red. I was wearing the huge hoop earrings he'd brought back from one of his work trips. He always came back with gifts.

I spent years looking at that photo, poring over the details. The moments leading up to it, and my mum walking up just after it was taken, holding her arms out to Carlo. She presented him with a snow globe that she'd bought from the gift shop at the Abbey – 'to add to your collection'. When Carlo had moved in he'd not brought that much stuff, but he'd lined the mantelpiece with snow globes. From Italy mostly, 'To remind me of home,' he said. My mum had teased him but studied them. Remembered. There was no surer stamp of approval. My sister raised her eyebrows and her forehead wrinkled in those symmetrical lines. It has never been in her nature to trust my boyfriends, especially after the messy ending with The Artist, but even she had a smile on her lips.

On my birthday evening we ate the worst curry I have ever had the misfortune to experience. No one complained. They were so happy for us. So pleased for me, so relieved, after what happened with The Artist. They just wanted us to enjoy our night, for nothing to dampen the mood. It was a celebration, after all.

On the evening of my family's visit, takeaway eaten and kids in bed, the three of us sit around the kitchen table again.

'I'll do something nice tomorrow night,' I said. 'Left it too late to start cooking the lasagne tonight. It's a bit of a fiddle.'

'Don't be daft, you! We'll go out for our dinner tomorrow night. We're on holiday.' My mum sounds worn out already.

My sister pours us all a fresh glass of wine, into clean glasses.

'Do the kids know anything?' my mum asks, and shakes her head slowly. 'I can't believe how big they're getting.'

'They don't know a thing – and I want to keep it that way. For as long as possible.'

My sister nods. 'God, yes, they're far too young to take this in.'

'So, the child that he had, the wee boy. Did he even exist?'

'He did, he was – is – his real son. He must be a teenager now. The picture on the bookcase, do you remember? That was really him.'

'And the sister?'

'Yes, that was also his real sister. The only picture he didn't have up was his real wife.'

A beat, a glance between them both. The last few weeks have involved so many disclosures, so many conversations. It's easy to forget who knows what.

'His what? His real wife?'

'Yes. He had an actual wife, Mum. The mother of his son, actually. He told me it was a fling. They lived in a house less than an hour from my flat in Maida Vale. She was pregnant with their second child when he lived with me. I've seen the birth certificate. She knew nothing about this. She would have thought he was at work. Saving the world from terrorists or drug gangs or something.'

'At work? For two years?!' My mum is crimson and the nail-tapping on the table is insistent now.

It all sounds so unreal. I need to explain to my family that the researchers showed me the birth certificates and the marriage certificate, all these details of Carlo's life. I don't know how to start, to lay out what's been happening. Each day a different revelation, though this one had caught my breath short.

Peter Salmon had called, making small talk. Awkward though. 'Donna, I have to tell you something and you're not going to like it,' he'd said, and I could have guessed. 'Carlo was married. We've checked it all out, every detail. They got married twenty-one years ago, had a child.'

I'd asked how they met. The first question to come to my lips. Peter had found their engagement notice in the newspaper. They'd met quite young, got engaged in their early twenties. As Peter told me the details I imagined this woman, who happily sent her husband off on his supposedly dangerous undercover missions. Wondered if she asked questions, scrutinised him like I should have done. Or perhaps she accepted things she shouldn't, overlooked warning signs. Like I did.

I'd looked her up on Facebook, while I was trying to find out his surname. My need to know his real identity was compulsive, almost obsessive. I had to name the ghost. It felt like some kind of validation rested on this truth-seeking mission. If I knew his real name, maybe I could lay his ghost to rest. Carlo Neri, the man who didn't exist. And the other Carlo, the state spy who was paid to lie and paid to sleep with me. Finding his real family had led to us finding him. This was just before his wife and the rest of the family were warned about Carlo being exposed in the press, and instructed to make their social media accounts private. This real wife looked nothing like me. Older, with blonde hair and an expensive real-holiday tan. I wonder if she looked me up too, if she was curious about the woman her husband secretly lived with for two years. The woman who had pictures of her son on her bookcase. I hadn't realised what it meant, the investigation into Carlo. That she would be told, would learn her life with Carlo was a lie. I hope she had family, her own, to sit around and talk it through with. I think about how the children must feel. The little boy whose picture was on the bookcase. I have seen from the photos that he is a young man now. He looks like his father.

My sister stares at her glass, slowly shaking her head. 'I can't take this in. I can't believe this has happened to you.' She looks suddenly lost. She is always in charge, so self-possessed. 'To think he came to my graduation.'

'Oh my God, yes! Do you remember, he stood up for the national anthem and he was told to sit back down?!'

'Yes! Charlie said to him, "What the hell are you doing, man?" His suit was a bit weird, don't you think? A bit middle-aged, staid?'

'Now you tell me! I do remember his shoes were always perfectly polished. Definitely a sign.'

We look at each other, laughing at how ludicrous it all is, finding some comfort in each other despite how awful the truth is.

'Snow globes.' My mum looks through the dark kitchen window, out into the small back garden. The solar fairy lights I put round the pear tree are just coming on.

'What's that, Mum?'

'Snow globes. Do you remember, he collected them? I used to buy them whenever he came to Scotland, from Arran or Largs, or Burns Cottage. Portugal even, if we went on holiday. He had dozens of them. Do you think he even liked snow globes?' Her eyes mist over. 'God, remember the time he looked after Sophie, while we were discussing what to do about Gran's headstone?

Was that not the same trip as the Stiff Little Fingers gig?

Yes. Carlo suggested that. It seemed like a long way to go for a gig.

He had decided we would go and see Stiff Little Fingers in Kilmarnock.

'We could just go and see them in Shepherd's Bush,' I'd said. 'Is it not a bit of a trek, all the way to Ayrshire for a gig?'

'Nah, I don't mind driving up there, darlin'. Some of the London anarchists are going up to Scotland. It means you get to see your mum and sis again. It's good for you to see as much of them as possible. Everyone is still grieving for your gran.'

The previous month, I had been due to fly to Florence to meet Carlo when I'd got the call from my mum.

'I don't think you should go to Italy, pet. I don't think she'll last that long.'

My gran had been in hospital for a couple of months by then and I had visited in the summer, sure that she would be going home. Now, when it became apparent she wouldn't be going home again, I changed my plans. I transferred my flight so our friend Joe could join Carlo in Italy, and I travelled home from London alone.

I spent four days with her before she died. On the first day she was fully lucid. She gave me a withering look, body tired but grey eyes still incisive.

'That's that,' she said, all matter-of-fact. 'My time must be up if you've cancelled your romantic week away in Italy with your new lumber.'

We had spent two days reminiscing. The time we went for high tea in Ayr with her friend Nancy, who wore fancy hats and had a flat in Wellington Square. Nancy was posh. I loved the big windows and the view to the sea. I must have been four or five. The incident at the Low Green pond, when Gran let me go out in a rowing boat by myself. I rowed myself around in circles in the middle of the pond till I cried, Gran becoming increasingly frantic at the side. I had to be rescued by a big ginger man with a frightening beard.

'You spoiled me rotten, didn't you?' I stroked her hand, wetting her lips every ten minutes, as she was barely taking fluids.

'Aye . . . we were always the best of pals.'

On the final day, she was seeing cabbages coming out of the walls, and imaginary children were giggling in her hospital room. I'll always associate cabbages with death.

A few weeks later, when Carlo and I arrived in Scotland for my sister's graduation, everyone was still dazed, and my mum in particular was raw and tearful. Carlo immediately blended in, looking after my uncle's granddaughter Sophie while we all argued, lovingly, about who would be paying what for the funeral, and debated the choice of headstone. A Celtic cross, in black granite, we decided by a democratic vote. Mum wanted a cheaper version. My uncle wanted to pay for the lot. There was a battle of prides going on. Carlo served us chilled glasses of Vermentino that he had brought in a mixed crate of fancy wines, to salve the mood.

Sophie was only three. She was the same age as the estranged son Carlo told me about. She took a real shine to Carlo. The previous time we were in Scotland, she had asked Carlo what stories he liked and he'd told her his favourite was about a little mole who went on a hunt for the owner of a mysterious poo. On this trip, he brought the book about the little mole as a present for her.

6

Husband Material

'Did you see that series, *Undercover*, about the woman who found out her husband was a police spy?'

Martin is one of the dog walkers I meet on the beach every day. His dog Charlie, a black-and-white cocker spaniel, is always subservient to my two springers. They are all ball fiends.

'Yes, good piece of drama.'

I root around in my coat pocket, searching for my lip balm. I have only just applied it. My lips were dry from biting them. It is an irritating habit.

'It reminds me of those women, you know the ones who sued the police. I heard about them on Radio 4.'

No one in my normal world has ever mentioned this. It feels uncomfortably close, encroaching on my delineated space. I push my fists deep into my Parka pockets. The sea is my sanctuary, untainted by the lies and the stench of police corruption. I say my goodbyes to Martin and Charlie and head for the quietest, furthest-away part of the beach, pulling my green hat down tight on my knotted hair until it almost covers my eyes. I have a hairdresser's appointment shortly. Amy will raise her eyebrows in mock alarm because my hair hasn't seen a brush for a week. 'I've been busy,' I'll laugh, putting my best face on.

Dogs walked, I fill their matching paw-print bowls with fresh water, offering a snack to each. They grab the earthy-smelling chews from my hands, narrowly avoiding my fingers, and slink off in separate directions. I wash my hands at the kitchen sink, then check the time on my phone. Two new messages. There is no signal at the wildest part of the beach. I don't want to talk to anyone, but I'd better check in case it's school.

'Hi, Donna, it's Alison. Just checking in to see how you're doing. Do you want to meet in London some time soon? Speak soon.'

I send a quick text message:

Yes, definitely. Will call. Off to hairdressers! Much love xxx

Running late now, I walk-run down the road, under the railway bridge that smells of piss, passing the chemist that dispenses all the methadone scripts, nipping around the side of Lidl for a shortcut. Not the most scenic but the quickest route. I narrowly avoid a speeding driver, who doesn't indicate before turning right, almost knocking me over.

'You stupid bitch!'

'Fuck you,' I yell back. 'Learn to drive!' I speed up as he reverses back down the road towards me. I can see a toothy black Staff in the back of the car, ready to rip a couple of my digits off. I run across the flashing traffic lights and onto the pedestrianised street. Narrow escape.

I crash into the salon, the door swinging shut behind me. Stand there, the few people in the room watching me.

'How have you been?' Amy raises one eyebrow and beckons me over. As I drop my bags on the floor she hands me her special de-knotting brush, normally reserved for small, furious children.

'Mad stuff, Amy. Batshit crazy, in fact.' I throw myself down on the chair, still out of breath from my encounter. I start laying out my phone, lip balm, notebook and pen on the small shelf attached to the mirror. *God, the dark circles under my eyes are terminal.*

I start brushing my hair as we both watch my reflection, inquiry in Amy's face. She doesn't live in Folkestone. And she is vegan. I can trust her.

'I found out my ex didn't really exist. I've been a bit preoccupied.'

'What? He didn't "exist"?' She now thinks I'm psychotic.

'He was an undercover police officer. The person I *thought* he was didn't exist. He told me he was a locksmith. He was spying on my friends the whole time.'

'What had you done?'

'Nothing! I was managing a drug treatment service for homeless people! I just went to work every day. Like you.'

Feeling a bit defensive. *I've done nothing wrong.*

'He was spying on my friends who were involved in the trade unions. I was a trade union rep too. All we gave a shit about was safety and workers' rights. Hardly a threat to the nation. We were campaigning against racism, against the far right. You've heard of Stephen Lawrence, right?'

She nods at me in the mirror, face long and serious.

'So the Lawrence family was spied on too. And the cops who investigated Stephen's murder colluded to let the killers go free. There's a whole scandal wrapped around political policing. They were a secret police unit, part of the Met.'

'Oh my God, Donna. How long were you with him?' The surprise in her face, the concern, it makes me want to curl up in the dark. I know other people in the room are listening now. Wish I hadn't said anything. But now I have, I can't stop. As though this anonymous space is a safe zone where I can say what I want.

'Two years. We got engaged. Turns out he was married the whole time.'

Carlo asked me to marry him on Hogmanay, just three months after that sunny day on Piccadilly when he was moody behind the dark glasses. He went down on one sturdy knee, unexpectedly, just before midnight.

We'd just spent Christmas apart, him in Italy and me in Scotland. We'd exchanged presents in bed before he dropped me to the airport to catch my Ryanair flight to Prestwick. He had carefully wrapped presents for each of my family.

As they all opened their presents from Carlo on Christmas Day, my mum said she wished Carlo was with us too.

Next year, I said. And Carlo promised we'd be together next year too, for sure.

It was Carlo who'd suggested a party, said we should do it properly, the Scottish way. He'd invited our whole gang, people from across the activist scene and a few others too. He'd been the one to make the calls, sending messages out. It was Carlo who bought the Christmas tree and decorations, and we'd put them up together the week before Christmas, tipsy on sparkly wine. Tinsel everywhere, fairy lights around the doorframe. We'd spent the day planning a playlist, sharing songs. As people arrived, we welcomed them with Rossinis, prosecco and blended strawberry. Carlo had blended the strawberries himself, said they were much better than Bellinis, and added fresh strawberry as a garnish. The guests filled our small flat, laughter bouncing off the walls.

Carlo was wearing the shirt my mum had bought him for Christmas, a pinky-beige cord affair with flowers. He moved around the room, saying hello to anyone he'd never met, pointing in my direction. I'd chat to friends, who'd each say, 'He's a keeper, that one.' Carlo would return to me each time, bringing me close to dance.

Not everyone present heard the proposal, as the party was in full flow. The Pogues were blasting out from the CD player. *I've got a feeling this year's for me and you.*

'*I love you, baby . . .*' he sang. 'Will you marry me, Donna?' On one knee in the middle of the dancefloor.

Looking down at his face, I knew he loved me. His eyes would never lie.

'Yes! Yes, I will marry you!'

I whooped and everyone turned around to see him effortlessly lift me off my feet, my black tights showing as my swirly Christmas dress got caught up in his arms. Our friends – Scottish, English, Spanish, Irish, Italian, Ethiopian, Maltese and the Chilean guy with the scars – hip-hip-hoorayed us with prosecco or peaty malt, and someone said we were made for each other.

He put me down, arms still wrapped around me, looking into my eyes.

'Let's ring your mum,' he said.

'We'll never get through! The lines will be busy with New Year phone calls.'

He pinched my waist, holding me tightly. 'Go on, darlin'. I want to tell her the good news.'

I had wanted to stay there swaying with him, holding that moment in time. But he pulled us out of the room, into the cold night. He took his phone out, dialling my mum's number before I could protest that we should sit under the stars together a few more moments. Her voice broke the silence of the night, then Carlo's, telling her the news. Her shouts of joy as Carlo wrapped an arm around me. Holding onto me.

* * *

Friday night. I've had my hair done just to sit in the house, kids fast asleep upstairs and dogs snoring at my feet. *Later . . . With Jools Holland* is on in the background, some irritating tinkly jazz thing. Not keen on jazz. I only like Chet Baker. I much prefer the blues. I mute the TV and reach for my laptop. Peter Salmon sent me a load more documents earlier – various things to review, corroborate, dispute. I left them in the email, shut the screen and tried to focus on my family. But now, in the quiet, they pull me back. I know I must add the new documents to my Dropbox file marked LEGAL. My cursor hovers over it, sitting between BANKING and PHOTOGRAPHS. Inside, the evidence of a full and happy life.

- Birth cert – Carlo
- Birth cert – daughter
- Birth cert – sister
- Birth cert – son
- Birth cert – wife
- Marriage certificate – with occupation

The marriage certificate is for his first wedding, his first wife. Their names twinned at the bottom of the page. They announced their engagement and their nuptials in *The Times*. Not so working-class after all. I bet they drank champagne, not the fizzy Lambrusco he promised me.

Soon after the Hogmanay proposal, Carlo told me he'd almost got engaged once before, in Italy. We had announced our engagement to everyone who wasn't at the party soon after New Year. Sitting around the pub with our friends, holding hands, it felt like an old-fashioned thing. They slapped us on the back and

Carlo ordered a round of drinks for everyone, pulling a wodge of notes out of his wallet to pay. Winking at me as he told the barmaid to take a drink for herself.

People were asking to see the ring, but there wasn't one yet. I didn't mind.

'Shall we go ring shopping together, then?' I asked him later that evening, lying in bed. He told me he needed to choose the ring himself but would seek advice from my sister. He might even take her shopping. This was news to me.

'It's the traditional Italian way!' he protested, as I poked him in the ribs.

'How will you know if it fits me?'

'A ring sizer, you div! You go into any jewellers and get fitted. Rings are a standard size, you know.'

'Christ, you seem to know a lot about engagement rings. Are you sure you haven't been engaged before?'

I eyed him suspiciously and he looked away. Then he turned back with a grin, a glint in his eye.

'Once . . . almost. She turned me down. Paola. She moved back to Brazil.' So lightly.

'*Ooh. Paola.* What was she like?' I disguised my jealousy by putting on a funny voice. Carlo hadn't mentioned her before.

'Typical Brazilian. She had a Brazilian.' He grabbed me by both thighs and pulled me onto him.

'Fuck Brazilians. I'm a feminist, don't you know? Why would I want to look like a prepubescent child? I'll shave my legs and pits and that's it!'

'I know you're a feminista,' he said, 'that's just one of the many reasons that I love you.'

He kissed me then, and the conversation ended. Sometimes I mentioned 'the Brazilian', and at first Carlo would make a joke, call me jealous. Later he'd snap, 'Jealousy doesn't suit you,' and I put her out of my mind.

Carlo has a new wife now, Peter Salmon has informed me. This appears to be an authentic relationship, it says in the spreadsheet he is keeping on Carlo, which I have access to. Genuine relationship.

I met her once, at a birthday party, early on in our relationship. She didn't look much like me. Small, mid-length brown hair, hardly any make-up. *The natural look.* Younger than me by a few years. I recognised her instantly; call it a sixth sense.

When I went to his flat in Hackney, that first weekend we met, there was a postcard from her on the fridge, from Australia. A message – funny, cautious, warm. I picked it up and read it a few times, then I felt his breath on my shoulder. He said he'd briefly dated her before he met me. He told me he would finish it with her. That it was only a casual thing. He took the card from me gently, laid it on the side and moved me to the sofa. I never saw the postcard again.

She was playing the saxophone at the party, I think. Or maybe it was the trumpet. It was a ska band. She was on stage, dressed in black and white with her ponytail swinging, glancing at Carlo every so often. I was dancing with Liam and I slipped and fell over. Everyone stared and Carlo shot me a sharp, judgemental look.

I shake my head as I replay this scene. It annoys me more than anything else. I have recently read a report by the researchers describing that relationship as 'genuine'. I recoiled at that word. Genuine. Genuine to whom? How could she be with him? Knowing what he was? She knew him both before and after. She knew all about his double life. She knew. His wife and I, we didn't.

I pour a glass of wine and put some folk music on. I decide to look at photos instead of watching TV, and open the file marked PHOTOGRAPHS. Carlo aged thirty-two. Except he was thirty-three. His birthday isn't 12 February, two days before Valentine's Day. His real birthday is in March. He was pretending to be an Aquarius. Carefree and socially conscious. I study him in this photo – red T-shirt, denim jacket, dark jeans. Sunglasses of course. He's leaning back against the wall, arms folded and watching the camera, a slight smile on his face. I don't even remember taking it, but then we took so many photos in the early days. I work my way through the photos, find one from a birthday. I'd bought him a cake and he grinned up from it at me.

When Peter Salmon first went looking for Carlo's records, he swore he saw a birth certificate that matched his cover name, Carlo Neri. When he went back to the central registry at St Catherine's House to order a copy it was gone. Apparently that happened a few times; as the net got tighter around the Met they covered their tracks even more carefully. Or perhaps it wasn't them; perhaps he acted alone. Perhaps Peter had never seen it.

I realise how much I have created a myth around Carlo over the years. He sits on a shelf marked The Lost Love of My Life. On that shelf are things he left, things he gave me, this file of photographs. I have a playlist of songs that remind me of him, and I listen to it still. This is a form of self-harm, I think. It's not healthy.

After Carlo moved out, I struggled to accept the severance because it felt like he was still there. His smell, that musky, earthy smell, would not leave me. It followed me around. I thought I was going mad in the days immediately after he left, even thinking he had been in the flat when I wasn't there. I would wander from room to room, checking if the cup on the draining board had moved, if the kitchen sink was dry or if the tap had been run since I left for work that morning. Once I tried to find a birthday card that he had given me and a photo of us together in Glasgow, which I was certain had been in my black keepsake box, but they seemed to have disappeared. Did he take them? I wondered. Maybe that shows his love for me. He might come back.

And he did come back. Two weeks after moving out, he called me and asked to meet up that evening. He picked me up from the flat at precisely seven-thirty. I could see out of the bay window that he had a new estate car, a blue one this time. He came to the door and rang the bell, which was strange.

'Don't you still have a key?'

'I didn't feel right just letting myself in.'

'You look a bit better,' I said. The scruffy hair had been trimmed and he'd shaved the huge mountain beard back to a neat goatee. He looked almost normal again.

'You look lovely,' he whispered before we left the house, engulfing me with all the desire that used to be there. He was coming back to me, I knew it. He turned back towards the car and I followed after him, dazed. Before we pulled away he put the radio on, and we sat in silence for the journey.

We had dinner in the fancy restaurant in Smithfield Market where everything is meat – 'nose to tail' they called it. It cost a small fortune, but he had booked it and insisted he was paying. During dinner he stroked my hand and called me 'darling' and behaved like a man about to propose marriage for the second time. I thought he might produce the engagement ring that had never materialised.

'I miss you so much. I need just a bit more time to sort my head out, and then we can find somewhere together.'

I told him I was moving in with my colleague Steve and his partner in Brixton for a few months, as I had been given notice to leave the flat. Said it cautiously, testing the water. He didn't raise any objections and I felt the deep hurt of disappointment.

'Back to south London for me.' I tried to sound jovial but there was no joy in my voice.

'That's excellent, darlin'. I'm relieved you've got somewhere. I'll help you move your stuff to Steve's.'

'Oh well, we're both moving in with our own Steves now!' I attempted feebly to lighten the mood. He didn't respond.

'How come you have a new car?' I asked.

'Work traded the other one in. They've given me a loan to buy a motorbike too. I'm going to buy you a jacket and a helmet next weekend when I get paid, and we can have some real adventures.'

We went back to the flat at the Barbican where he was staying temporarily. 'I'm going to show you a trick,' he said. We got in the lift.

'I can take us right to the top of the building. There's a way of fiddling the lift – I'll show you.'

We went up to the top floor and stopped, then he did something to the panel, and we went up again.

'It's a secret floor. Come on, I'll show you.'

On the top we looked out over all of London at night.

'Oh my God, Carlo, this is so beautiful! How do you know these things?'

He put both hands around my waist and pulled me tight to him. He was as hard as a rock.

'Secrets,' he said, 'I know lots of secrets.'

It was the most intense feeling I'd ever known. Pushing against the dark London night. No barriers, no defences. I could have fallen.

All of the city beneath us. Him, a shadow, below, behind, inside.

A little death, whispering out into dark London.

The next morning, I was wrapped up in white sheets and the autumn sun was scattered in a pattern on the bed. He handed me a paper bag; inside a book. *The Reader* by Bernhard Schlink. The book is about a young man's relationship with an older woman in post-war Germany. It is about memories and remembrance. And pain.

'You'll love this,' he said. 'It's a tough read, but you will get it.'

He dropped me off home, kissed me on the step, pushing me just slightly against the closed door. I stayed there until his car had disappeared, holding the book against my chest.

Carlo Neri does not exist. Carlo Neri does not exist. Carlo Neri does not exist.

I was in love with a fiction, a character straight out of a book. I come back to this again and again at times like this, when it's 1 a.m. and I'm still wide awake, nursing a glass of red wine, dogs beside me on the settee. Was there really a child? Stealing the identities of the dead was a common practice amongst the special demonstration squad. Maybe there was a wee boy called Carlo who died at the age of three or four.

I have become obsessed with the details, the truths that I can hold onto, good or bad. 'They had to be married,' Alison had said, 'to make sure they went back. A stable base.'

The irony of it. From what I had heard, none of the undercover police officers had stayed married. The wives had been duped, just like us. I don't know how many married again, rebuilt a happy life. How many were taking new photos, building new memories. Like Carlo.

The first time I went home to Ayrshire after finding out about Carlo, my uncle asked me, 'What about the dead children?'

He wasn't the only one to zone in on that. People are disgusted by this aspect of the story. They are right to be disturbed. It was first in the news when they found out about the little boy who died in a plane crash. Eight years old. His identity was stolen by a well-spoken man in his thirties called James. An undercover cop a little too James Bond, slipping into the scene like a champagne socialist. Wearing the name of a dead boy with pride. Doing his duty. But this was not a sick one-off. It was common practice, a directive given to new recruits. An undercover officer's first task was to spend hours and hours at the family records centre in St Catherine's House, leafing through the death registers in search of a fairly bland name he could take as his own. They would share a first name. It is much harder to maintain a false first name. If you're called John and someone shouts 'James' in the street, you don't automatically turn around.

When I was a child, I was fascinated by dead children. Local dead children, that is. I knew of two. One eight-year-old boy who was kicked and then trampled by a horse. A gang of kids were trying to jump on its back and this poor wee bugger ending up getting the force of the horse's fear. I knew the boy's sister. And his mum. It was only the two of them, no dad was ever mentioned. They lived in an upper maisonette just around the corner from us.

The other dead child haunted me. She had been the same age as me and she lived around the corner too, but in the other direction. She was called Jeanette. Her mum was an alcoholic and Jeanette used to get sent to the shop to ask for bread, milk and cigarettes on tick. The family that owned the wee shop were good-hearted, letting people run up to five pounds of debt before they clamped down. But they never said no to a child, and some parents exploited this generosity.

The story of Jeanette's life, and death, haunted me because I had seen her face. In real life. Then on the front of the *Ayrshire Post* after she died. Jeanette was killed by her older brother. He repeatedly jumped on her stomach, causing fatal internal injuries. Their mother was not at home at the time.

When I first heard the story, I couldn't get it out of my head. The image of her face intruded on my waking life and also forced its way into my dreamscape – horrifyingly distorted versions of her. The girl lying on her bed, being attacked by her big brother. I had never been in their house, but I visualised the bedroom. The mattress was stained, with no bottom sheet. I had seen their house from the outside. A scruffy four-bedroom house, an overgrown garden with odds and sods of rubbish and broken furniture strewn about. The curtains were a murky yellow, only half-hung, with gaps like missing teeth.

Jeanette was only eight when she died; her brother the murderer was fifteen. He was sentenced to life imprisonment, to serve a minimum of twenty years. I asked my uncle if he knew what had happened to the rest of the family. He said the other two kids were taken into care. The mother died while still in her forties. The boy would now be a man and would have served his time. He'd be out of jail. Did he have a new name? I wondered. Did he go on to have children of his own?

'Where is Jeanette buried?' Prestwick Cemetery, my uncle told me. Where Bridget, my gran, is. And my granny and grandpa on the other side too. I wondered how many people still remembered

Jeanette, how many people searched for her likeness in photos. And I wondered how many people looked for signs of a little boy. If anyone saw his name in a paper next to Carlo's photo. The jolt they'd feel to see it, next to a man who'd be the same age he would have been. Perhaps they thought for just a second that he'd lived. Remembered that couldn't be true and thought how strange, what a coincidence, to share a name.

I felt such a strong wave of grief that I wept. Tidal waves of tears. Snot pouring from me. It was strangely cathartic. I rarely cried these days.

7

Ghosts

During Rob's trip to Folkestone to interview me for the big *Guardian* story, I agreed to speak to the man from the BBC, Richard Watson, who had also been working on the scoop. Their plan is to make a short film for *Newsnight*, which will be aired on the same evening that the *Guardian* story is published. Both will reveal Carlo to be an undercover cop, telling my story to the world. Everyone seems keen for me to get involved and I get a friendly email from Richard, asking if we can arrange a call.

I'm walking along the cliffs when he calls, holding my mobile to my ear as I look out at the sea. Richard explains the process for the recording, matter-of-fact about the steps required. He is encouraging, but I get the feeling he doesn't often get turned down.

If I get involved it will mean a few day trips to London and potentially lots of filming, for a twenty-minute news feature. I mull it over as I walk home, and when I get there I call Alison to ask what she thinks.

'You should do it,' she says, 'if you feel up to it. But speak to Harriet first. One of us can come with you, remember.'

'Don't worry, I can manage on my own.' Not a thought for the consequences, as usual.

'Will you come to Kilburn next week? We can chat properly then. My friend Kefi Chadwick is doing a read-through of her play at the Tricycle. You'll get to meet some of the others there too. Lisa is definitely coming, and Belinda.'

Lisa is the activist who had a long relationship with Mark Kennedy. She unmasked him when she found his passport in the glove compartment of the car when they were on holiday. This started the whole chain of events that led to the eight women bringing their case. That chance discovery is what led to the Undercover Policing Inquiry. It's what led to Carlo being exposed. I've wanted to meet Lisa for a long time.

'Yes, I would love to come. You know I lived in Maida Vale, with Carlo?' I'm aware that my voice sounds flat. Memories flood my consciousness. The flat on Elgin Avenue, a black motorbike parked outside. I remember the only time Carlo really lost his cool was when the bike got a parking ticket. He was so flustered. Now I realise why. The ticket would have been sent to his real address. His *genuine* family home.

I shiver involuntarily at the memory of Kilburn. I'd not been to that part of London for a decade. Carlo and I had been to the Tricycle many times to watch plays and films, radical-left Italian arty things. We went to see *Salò* by Pasolini, and a documentary about Chilean musician Victor Jara, murdered by the fascist Pinochet regime. Afterwards we would eat in a cute French restaurant on Kilburn High Road, a dark, romantic place where Edith Piaf sang to us to not have any regrets and our limbs would join seamlessly together under the small table, intimate touches masked by the ubiquitous red-and-white checked tablecloth. We would walk the leisurely ten minutes back down the Edgware Road in the cool darkness to our cosy flat in Maida Vale, and then nestle together in bed, planning our future wedding and naming our future children and our future dog. Luca and Frida were our favourite human names, and the scruffy rescue hound would wear a red bandana and there was no dispute that he would be named Che.

On the other end of the line, Alison is delighted. 'I'm so glad you're coming to this, Donna. It will be good for you.' I know she wants me to be more involved, more tightly enmeshed. I didn't go to see the play, *Any Means Necessary*, when it premiered in Nottingham, but it had five-star reviews and I have already met Kefi Chadwick, the playwright, briefly, at a demo outside the Royal Courts of Justice. She is part of the extended campaign gang and I am part of that gang now too, one of the women. I get invited to everything they do as a group. A few weeks ago, they asked me to join them for the Metropolitan Police's apology to the eight women, which was going to be headline news. I would have loved to go but had already made plans to go to Scarborough for a short break with Tania.

It was surreal, watching the wholehearted apology by Assistant Commissioner Martin Hewitt on the BBC in the frilly dining room of the Grand Hotel overlooking Scarborough Bay. Hewitt was dressed in full uniform and speaking seriously to the camera. Press camera flashes were bursting and shutters snapping loudly. He said that what happened was terrible and it would never happen again, and he said the officers involved abused these women's human rights. Then there was Harriet speaking, my lawyer. And Helen. And Belinda, who had also waived her anonymity. She was deceived into a relationship by Bob Lambert, the notorious Debenhams firebombing agent provocateur.

Lambert is one of the most controversial undercover officers. He infiltrated animal rights and environmental campaigns in the 1980s and admits to having had relationships with four women while undercover. Lambert fathered a child with an activist named Jacqui before disappearing at the end of his operation, leaving his partner and child behind.

Lambert was unmasked in 2011 following investigations by the *Guardian* and campaigners he had infiltrated. Activists convicted of the firebomb attacks on three branches of Debenhams in 1987 believe that Lambert planted one of the devices.

Belinda would be at the reading of Kefi's play in Kilburn. I would be meeting more new people. The past few weeks had been a whirlwind of faces and stories, all interconnected, mandala-like. Half of me wanted to reach in and hold each of them, the other half wanted to run.

Sitting watching these faces on screen, knowing they'd wanted me to stand there with them, felt like seeing sliding doors. I looked down at my hands clenching the armrest.

'How are you feeling?' Tania had asked, more gently than usual. 'Really, I mean? Don't put on a face for me.'

'I feel like my neck and jaw will break if I move my head, I'm so tense. My skull feels like there's an axe embedded in it and my left eye is on fire. I really want a drink, or a diazepam.'

'I've not got any drugs, as well you know, lady. Go on, just have a wee beer, you're on your holidays. What do you want? I'll get it.'

'Oh, go on, make it a pint, please. Anything Mediterranean. No Budweiser pish.'

That pint had been followed by another, by talk of old times and no mention of Carlo. Tania had wanted to draw me out of it, wanted to make me laugh. We had laughed as well, making each other giggle bringing up old tales of vintage outfits, crazy days at work, bad behaviour by various men, late nights listening to David Bowie and Sunday-morning veggie breakfasts in the local greasy spoon.

'Remember that time Buffalo Bill called us a pair of miserable cunts?'

'In the Sun and Doves? How could I forget?! That was because I wouldn't change the minutes of a union meeting. Imagine the brass neck of him, asking me to falsify union minutes? Whose leaving do was that?'

'Oh, some wee lassie. Cannae mind her name. He was like an octopus, tentacles all over the place.'

'At least he never grabbed our thighs!'

'Aye, I'd rather be called a cunt than groped by him, any day!'

Buffalo Bill was our senior manager, with an eye for the ladies and a ruthless streak. He wasn't happy with Tania and me not bending to his demands. He grudgingly gave me a good reference when I left for another job.

We'd laughed ourselves dizzy at these memories, hugging each other tightly before going to bed in the faded, scruffily elegant family suite of the Grand Hotel, Tania warning me not to snore as she climbed under the quilt.

I'd stayed looking out of the window for a while. The moon reflected onto the black sea below, a distorted face. Tania was already snoring by the time I climbed into the bed beside her.

I meet Richard Watson from the BBC for the first time at his flat in Camberwell. This is a slightly unusual meeting venue, but Richard explains on the phone that he has mobility issues. Camberwell is my old barrio, I tell him, very happy to come to you. I can catch up with an old friend after our meeting.

I collect all the photos together that I've been able to find, printing off ones I only had digitally. My mum has kept more pictures than me, sending me an endless stream of happy holiday photos. Carlo and me, arm in arm across two years, my mum eager behind the camera.

Once I've put the photos in a file, I start collecting the gifts, taking letters from the box under my bed, rooting out the jewellery. I am convinced that personal belongings went missing from my flat after Carlo moved out.

I travel down to Camberwell, crawling through traffic on the Walworth Road. Richard has a beautiful flat, only a short walk from the chaos of the green. He greets me at the door, tall, confident, in a shirt and casual trousers. I admire the architecture and the artwork, and he responds lightly, used perhaps to this sort of response. The small talk is brief, and with a cup of jasmine tea in hand we settle down to flick through my mini archive of life with Carlo. Richard asks me question after question. *Where was this? And when was this? Who was this person? Why were you there? Who decided where to go?*

A deluge of questions. I am beginning to feel like a robot. My answers are becoming devoid of any feeling. I've had Rob ask me lots of questions for the newspaper article, and the undercover researchers and activists asked so many questions at the beginning. My lawyer asked lots of questions for my witness statement, to be used for my civil claim against the police. It will be launched on the same day that the news story goes live.

It is all a big scoop. My case is the first to come to light since the eight women settled and it will make the headlines for sure. Richard says after the massive apology it surely will be a slam dunk that I'll settle my case quickly. Rob said the same the day he came to visit. I try not to think about money. How do you compensate someone for living with a ghost?

As Richard looks at the photos, asks questions about the jewellery, I find myself becoming quieter, my fingers tapping against the sofa edge. My concentration is drifting again.

To break the silence, I decide to tell Richard about the Illy espresso set. I remember when this gift appeared. Carlo had been in Modena on a work trip and had arrived home before I got in from work. The double lock wasn't on, and my heart lifted to know he was already waiting for me behind the door.

He pounced on me in the hallway. 'Close your eyes.'

'Why? What will you do to me?'

His hands, covering my eyes. His smell, the only smell I wanted. My love, home again after five days in Italy. Home before me. The door already unlocked. My journey across the city had been too long, and I was impatient. Bus stops on the way to the Elephant and Castle, far too many. The raving preacher man, a regular, but much too loud today. The Bakerloo line shuddering along, with its ancient carriages. But he was already with me. I could smell him, even before he was with me.

He pulled me into the bedroom. There was a box placed in the centre of the bed, wrapped in delicate paper. White with a silver bow.

'Open it, then. Go on!' His dark eyes twinkling, responding to my pleasure.

Cross-legged on the bed, I leaned over to unfasten the silver ribbon. 'From Modena?'

'You'll see.'

Careful not to tear the paper, so I could keep it, I gently prised the edges apart. Underneath, a plain white box. Lifting the lid, floaty tissue paper covered in stars, then six tiny cups and saucers.

'Oh my God! This is it!' I leaned back onto him as he climbed behind me on the bed. 'I can't believe you found it.'

The Illy espresso set. I had spotted it in Paris. It was 1999, and I was on holiday with The Artist. We saw it in the Picasso

Museum shop. It cost a hundred and thirty euros. Too much, he'd said. I'd wanted it ever since. I'd even looked for it on the internet, searching for it in French. It was a limited-edition set, one of an annual artist collection sets the coffee company released. And Carlo had found it and brought it home for me.

'I can't believe you found it. I love it. I'll treasure this for the rest of my life!'

I recently looked it up on eBay. Three hundred pounds, it's worth now. I told the other women this, laughing. Helen was shocked.

'All I got was a propagator!' she spluttered.

'Oh no, I got designer gear, sunglasses, long boots, jewellery. Talk about champagne socialism . . . all on Special Branch expenses!' I laughed at the absurdity of it.

Now I use the cups for salad dressings and garnishes for meals, and the saucers have become mini paint palettes for the girls. It's not a special gift any more. It is domestic, part of my so-called normal life.

I remember another day, in the spring of 2003 (it was light in the evening and things were still good between Carlo and me). I came home to find a vintage dressing table in our bedroom. It was huge, walnut, Art Deco, with triple mirrors.

'Where did you find this?' It was totally unexpected.

'On a job in Hampstead, darlin'. Customer was getting rid of it.'

'How did you get it into the flat?' It was solid.

'One of the lads from work gave me a hand.'

'You didn't manage to get this in the car?' I was becoming confused.

'No, we had a van today. Industrial-sized coffee machine being fitted.'

I'd never heard him mention a work van before.

As I sit in Richard Watson's airy living room, I suddenly wonder what the real story was behind that Art Deco dressing table. It occurs to me it might have been his wife's, a family heirloom. I feel sick at this thought and a cloud looms over me. I sit still until it passes. Gifts from old lovers have no hold over me.

I arrange to meet Richard again in a couple of weeks, for two full days of filming. One day is booked for a posh, members-only club in Kensington and the next day will be on location in Maida Vale. Richard is planning to drive around the area, scouting for good locations. We will probably film outside my old flat and possibly in the little café on the corner, where I used to eat bagels with scrambled eggs and smoked salmon and drink strong coffee, if it's still there. The team will consist of Richard, a cameraman and a producer called Maria. They will take care of me.

As I leave Richard's house, I call an old friend who still lives in Camberwell.

'Can you meet me for an hour? I'm done with the journalist.'

I have begun to realise that whenever I have these meetings, filled with probing questions about the past, the smell of it clings to me and it makes me feel nauseous. I need an hour or two to decompress before going home to my children, to cleanse myself of the stench of the corruption of the Metropolitan Police. I need this space so I can be normal, attentive Mummy again, not the distant stranger I feel myself becoming.

One of the kids tugged at my sleeve a few days before my last visit to London, when I was preoccupied by an email. 'What's wrong, Mummy, why don't you smile any more?'

'Don't I, darling?' I smiled distractedly.

'That's not a real smile,' she said, her own turning down at the sides. I'd swooped her up, dangling her backwards, taking all my strength. But when she'd run off again I was back looking at the email, considering whatever news it was imparting.

That evening I meet the friend in a nearby pub. She doesn't know about the case, never met Carlo. We talk about family, the strains of work and life unfolding. I tell her about my kids, describe their differences, revel in their successes. It's a make-believe, a return to three months previously. As I travel home it all comes flooding back, my temporary refuge dissolved. Richard's questions play over and over in my mind.

The Kilburn read-through of Kefi's play is emotionally charged. People in the row in front of me are crying. The audience is full of activists, survivors, victims of police cruelty. Aidan, who is a key character in the play, is in tears. He is a leading environmental activist and was close friends with Mark Kennedy before he was unmasked. He's a big man, and I have only ever seen him fierce or jokey, never like this. His shoulders are shaking, and his hand is held over his eyes. I'm sitting on my own, having slid in just before the curtain went up. I got to the venue early enough, but saw the crowds chatting around the bar and went for a walk, returning when the space had emptied.

The play is about Mel, a Nottingham activist, and her partner Dave, a carpenter. Carpenter, locksmith, candlestick maker. All these imagined jobs. Men's jobs. I suppose they thought the women would fall for men with a set of skills. Watching Mel and Dave on stage, their falling in love, it's a strange mirror. Not like me and Carlo, not different either. I can't take my eyes off them.

After the read-through, the actors join the audience in the foyer for drinks. I sit hesitantly to the side, on a chair pushed against the wall, taking it all in. I see Harriet, talking intently to Helen. Alison in another corner, laughing with two other women. The men by the bar. An older woman sits beside me. I didn't recognise her, but as soon as she says her name I know why she's here. Celia Stubbs. Her partner, Blair Peach, was attacked by the police on 23 April 1979 in Southall, west London, where I had worked for a while. Southall was a predominantly Sikh area and Blair – a popular young primary school teacher from New Zealand – had been on a march against fascism when the Special Patrol Group of the Metropolitan Police murdered him. Blair was a member of the National Union of Teachers and a committed socialist. Just before he died, he had been elected as the president of East London Teachers' Association.

An eyewitness account describes Blair Peach being attacked by approximately twenty riot cops from the Special Patrol Group, who were running towards him carrying riot shields and black truncheons. He saw one of them hit Blair on the head. The police moved off and left Blair sitting against the wall. He tried to get up, but he couldn't stand. Then the police came back and told him to move. They were very rough with him despite it being obvious he was seriously injured.

Blair Peach was taken to hospital by ambulance and had emergency neurosurgery for a large haematoma, but his condition worsened during surgery. He died in the early hours of 24 April.

No police officer was ever charged with his murder. In 2010 the Metropolitan Police Commissioner Sir Paul Stephenson agreed to reveal a report written by Commander John Cass, written after Blair Peach's death. All of the police officers' names were redacted and the language was heavily biased against the people attending the demonstration.

Cass states in the report:

My brief is to investigate the circumstances surrounding the death, so I do not propose to enlarge much further on the events of that day except to emphasise that it was an extremely violent, volatile and ugly situation where there was serious disturbance by what can be classed as a 'rebellious crowd'.

The legal definition 'unlawful assembly' is justified and the event should be viewed with that kind of atmosphere prevailing. Without condoning the death, I refer to Archbold 38th edition para 2528: 'In case of riot or rebellious assembly the officers endeavouring to disperse the riot are justified in killing them at common law if the riot cannot otherwise be suppressed.'

Celia Stubbs is also a core participant in the public inquiry into undercover policing. The home secretary Theresa May announced the inquiry following the police apology, to investigate this massive anti-democratic scandal, which encompassed us, the women deceived into relationships, as well as people like Celia; Stephen Lawrence's parents Doreen and Neville; the blacklisted workers Dave Smith and Steve Hedley, and many, many others. I am inextricably part of this surreal world now.

'How did you find the play?' asks Celia. 'I thought it was hugely moving.' She speaks softly, clearly.

'I feel a bit shaken, to be honest,' I reply. 'I haven't been back to this area since Carlo . . . We lived just down the road in Maida Vale and we used to come here, quite regularly, to this theatre, to see films.'

'Oh no, dear . . .' She gently pats my hand, her wise blue eyes locked with mine in solidarity. 'How long have you known?'

'I found out about three months ago.' I shake my head. 'I didn't have a clue for over ten years.'

'It must be devastating,' she says, mirroring my head-shake, 'but we must keep fighting. For the truth. We must make sure it never happens again.'

She's steely. More so than me, and I nod along encouragingly. But I'm not sure I want to fight, and I'm certainly not convinced this fight is going to stop this happening again. As I look at the room of passionate friends and allies I want to be a part of it, but it's just fifty people or so and I know what they're up against. I say a polite goodbye to Celia, promise to keep in touch and make my exit.

I arrive dead on time for the first day of filming at the Polish private members' club in South Kensington. I have managed to get an emergency hair appointment. 'The back is more important than the front,' I said to Amy. 'They can't film my face, so please make the back of my head look gorgeous!'

I wear a beautiful dress, an intricate William Morris pattern with a fitted top and flouncy skirt, black tights and heeled boots.

The room that is booked for filming has high ceilings and wooden floors, stark white walls and carefully placed arrangements of white flowers, with a massive ornate mirror on the wall. It makes a perfect film set. I'm introduced to everyone, and am surprised at how many people it takes to film a short video. Richard is attentive, careful to make sure I have everything I need. I have coffee and cake before we start, which I quickly realise is a bad idea as the coffee and the nerves set my tummy off. Three trips to the toilet before we begin.

By the end of the day, I want to kill the cameraman. The interview is easy enough, as I've told Richard the whole story already, but the cameraman wants to do fifteen retakes for every bloody shot.

'He's a perfectionist,' whispers Maria, the producer.

'He's an arsehole,' I mouth back at her and she grins. We clicked as soon as we met.

Day two of filming starts in the most gruelling way. I had arranged to meet Richard and his dictatorial cameraman in a café next to the tube station in Maida Vale. Elgin Avenue. The café is still there. It's where I went for breakfast with Carlo, and the corner shop next door is where we bought fresh bread, hummus, olives and falafel. Everything reminds me of him. I wonder if the video shop where we rented our indie films and where we once saw Björk is still there. The journey to Maida Vale from King's Cross on the Underground has been a lesson in survival. I am already aching from head to toe from yesterday's filming, from trying to sit in fixed positions while not looking stiff at all, and being barked at by the cameraman.

The second leg of the journey, changing from the Hammersmith and City to the Bakerloo line, hits me like a punch in the throat. As soon as we draw close my eyes start to blur, my hearing is fuzzy, I feel faint, and I begin to retch, grasping the seat to try to maintain my balance. The smears on the train windows and the orange-and-brown patterns on the seats turn gruesomely psychedelic. I must change at Baker Street and that nearly finishes me off. I have not been back to Baker Street Underground station since someone tried to push me under a train here. It happened soon after Carlo left me, when he lived in the Barbican flat but we were still seeing each other. The British Transport Police investigated the assault, but never found the man, though he had been captured on CCTV.

I had been at the Barbican, not with Carlo but with my work friend Lucy, to see a film called *21 Grams*. Afterwards we had gone for dinner. I was telling her how unhappy I was with the current state of things. The unexplained disappearances, the poor communication. Carlo was away that weekend, had told me he was visiting his sister. I'd texted a few times but got no response. I left Lucy at around eight-thirty to head back to Maida Vale and she went north to Finchley. As I went down the escalator towards the platform, I saw a man ascending the other escalator, to the station. He was staring straight at me, through me. His eyes were strange. I could only describe it as hatred. Burning into me. I'd never seen him before in my life.

I bowed my head to look down, shaking off the feeling of discomfort. A random lunatic, I reassured myself. I reached the bottom of the escalator and turned towards the platform, walking slowly. A train was coming in, the platform quiet for this time of the evening. I took a couple of steps and then suddenly I was punched hard, from behind. The blow landed right in the middle of my back. I fell to the floor, sliding forward from the force of the punch. The train pulled in and my head arrived just at the yellow line. When the doors opened a woman was standing there, shocked but not frozen. She had clearly seen it all and she pulled me up and into the carriage, looking over my head. I stared around the platform, but the man had gone. A few blurred faces looked at me as the train pulled away, frozen in inaction. The woman held my arm, told me I should speak to the train officer, asked if I knew the man. I shook my head, let her guide me off the train at the next stop and to the station staff. That interview, the feeling of telling the story so soon after it had happened, it left me shaken for weeks. I'd wanted more than anything to call Carlo, for him to come and get me, put his arms around me. Somehow, I didn't think I could. I didn't leave my house for several days.

* * *

Now, on the journey to meet the people from the BBC, to tell my story about Carlo, a decade later, it's as if my unknown assailant has returned. The physical threat feels real. Another ghost from my past, turning up uninvited, to haunt me after all these years. I can see his face and feel those burning eyes.

A flashback. My God, this is a flashback.

It is visceral, like he is physically here. The violence of this intrusion is too much, and I almost turn back. I want to go home, to my dogs, to close my front door on the world, to be anywhere else but here in west London, with all my ghosts jostling for their turn to haunt me.

8

The Reveal

After the film for BBC *Newsnight* is edited and approved, life becomes a waiting game. I return home, try to be in the present with my girls. Cinema trips and days on the beach, picnics in the park and attention. They revel in it, while I try to suppress the anxiety, the expectation of the next move.

I'm lying in bed one Sunday morning, papers scattered around me, when an email comes in from Harriet Wistrich, the subject line 'draft claim letter'. I open it on my phone. A note from Harriet, saying she'd like my view before formalising the draft and will wait to hear before she sends it.

I've been waiting for this moment. After that first meeting with Harriet we've been in touch frequently. Not with the devotion of friends like Tania, or the deep interest of people like Helen and Alison. But over the last few months she's checked in, kept me up to date. Alison and Helen were right about getting a lawyer; from that first meeting I've felt in safe hands. I've let go, just a little, the responsibility. When I gave her the witness statement she'd said, 'Leave it with me, Donna, just concentrate on yourself,' and I'd left her office not thinking much about it.

As I've shared facts with Peter Salmon and the other men, stories with Rob and Richard, feelings with Alison and Helen, Harriet has shared with me only what I needed to know. She and her team have investigated every small lead or clue, building a case that has fed into the wider police inquiry. I have been fighting to get through each day, and she has been fighting for me.

This email is the start of the end of her inquiries. Or maybe it is the end of the beginning.

18 January 2016

Dear Sirs

Re: Letter Before Claim on behalf of Andrea

We write on behalf of our above-named client who has recently been awarded Core Participant Status in the forthcoming undercover policing public inquiry under the category of 'Relationships'. On a purely confidential basis we are providing Andrea's real name, which is Donna McLean, born on 30 March 1972 in Scotland. She has recently discovered that a man she knew by the name Carlo Neri, with whom she was in a long-term intimate sexual relationship between 2002 and 2004, was in fact an undercover police officer whose real name is Carlo ■■■■■■■■. As you know, we have represented eight other women who were involved in such relationships, which led to the recent settlement (on behalf of seven of them) and public apology from the Assistant Commissioner. We set out below the circumstances and relevant facts giving rise to this claim and the legal basis on which this claim is brought and an indication of damages sought.

There is no turning back from this point. The moment I confirm with Harriet, I become a 'case'. I have agreed with Harriet that my claim against the Metropolitan Police will be launched on the same day that the *Guardian* article and the TV piece go live.

Harriet said it will have more impact. I trust everything she says. She's not just a lawyer, she's an activist too. Her firm, Birnberg Peirce, was established by the inimitable Gareth Peirce, one of the most successful human rights/activist lawyers on the planet. When I stop and think about this it blows my mind.

Harriet is an awe-inspiring character, with an infectious laugh and a formidable mind. She has been a solicitor for twenty-five years and founded the Centre for Women's Justice. She has won numerous awards for her groundbreaking human rights work and has acted in many high-profile cases involving violence against women. As well as representing our group of women deceived in relationships by undercover police officers, Harriet has taken on cases challenging the police and parole board in the John Worboys case and acts on behalf of women appealing murder convictions for killing abusive partners.

Finally, the broadcast date arrives. Monday, 18 January 2016. The letter before claim is sent in the afternoon, confirmed by email. The *Guardian* article goes live online at 6 p.m. and will be published in hard copy tomorrow.

I have group work this evening, not that I can really concentrate. Mindfulness. I laugh at the irony. I'm permanently mindless. One of the group members asks me if I'm okay. He says I don't seem myself tonight.

'Just a wee bit distracted, Jim. Kids, family, you know?'

Jim and the others nod sympathetically. They seem subdued too. My mood is clearly impacting on them. I feel guilty. I wonder if any of them will watch *Newsnight*. Someone might recognise my frock. I bought it from a small boutique in town, on the Old High Street. My hairdresser will recognise me if she tunes in. I was asked by the producer if I wanted an actor to voice my words.

No way, I said, that is so inauthentic. A wig? No way, I'm getting my hair done specially. This is the risk I am willing to take.

The group seems to drag on forever. At the end of the session Paul, anxious about seeing his mother for the first time in a year, wants to talk. I try not to look at the clock and mentally give him an extra five minutes. Once I've reassured him and gently ushered him out of the door I lock up the basement, setting the alarm on autopilot. I rush home, a hastily purchased bottle of Chilean fair-trade red from the Co-op shoved in my work bag, squashing down the Sharpie pens and the Post-it notes. I decide not to buy Italian wine for this occasion.

Mine is going be the first story featured on *Newsnight* this evening. Well, Andrea's story; that pseudonym. The kids sneak downstairs when they hear the front door. My task now is to get them back to bed as smoothly as possible. Their mission is to stay up as late as possible.

We sit around the table a while, and I try to tire them out with chatting about their day. After a bit I persuade them into their pyjamas, shuffling them into their shared bedroom.

'It's late,' I whisper as I tuck them in, one hugging a giant toy butterfly, the other one a panda.

'No, Mummy, you're the one who's late! Can you sing us "Ally Bally Bee"?'

This is their favourite Scottish lullaby, sung to me by my mum and my granny when I was the same age.

Ally bally, ally bally bee,
Sittin' on yer mammy's knee,
Greetin' for anither bawbee,
Tae buy some Coulter's Candy.
Here's auld Coulter comin' roon'

Wi' a basket on his croon
So here's a penny, noo ye rin doon
And buy some Coulter's Candy.

They smile up at me sleepily, all forgiven.

'Right, that's your lot! Sleep time, darlings.'

I extract myself, moving slowly backwards like a soldier on special ops, leaving the bedroom door ajar to provide some light from the hallway. They won't sleep in the pitch dark. I've started leaving a lamp on for myself, as the nightmares have been going on since the panic attack on the Bakerloo line. I'm no longer seeing images of the man who assaulted me, but occasionally I have vivid, horribly intrusive thoughts about Carlo. This has become something else to bear. I feel like I'm carrying extra mental weight all the time. It's exhausting.

I settle down in front of the TV at last, glass of wine in hand. As the *Newsnight* titles appear on the screen and the intro music plays, all I can see on the giant screens above the presenter Emily Maitlis's head is my enormous hand, green-painted nails clutching the photo of Carlo in the red T-shirt. I can't help but laugh, incongruously.

The phone starts pinging messages at me immediately.

Oh wheesht, I mutter, *let me watch it in peace.*

The opening scene takes place under the bridge at Little Venice, as I stand canal-side, clutching the iron railings. Throughout the film my face is disguised by either filming the back of my head or filming front-on in shadow.

We then move on to my interview in the fancy members' club in South Kensington. It is the perfect setting; I'm pleased with the contrast between my dark floral dress and my new smart hairdo set against the stark white walls. I come across as a calm and reasoned individual. Normal. The cameraman that I called a prick has done something clever and made my legs look longer and slimmer. I decide I like him after all.

My snapshots have been cleverly Photoshopped together into an album and Richard Watson and I flick through them as we talk about how Carlo came into my life and how he left it. Richard talks about the cynical escape strategy put together by Carlo and the Metropolitan Police, weaving a backstory of sexual and domestic abuse through our relationship in order for Carlo to break down and disconnect from me, physically and emotionally.

Although I had been rigid and in jaw-aching pain when we filmed, at one or two points in the fifteen-minute film I start giggling; when I explain that Carlo's disguise was a locksmith and then point out that he helpfully suggested home security improvements to half of the activists in London and subsequently changed their locks. Carlo had the key to my heart. Special Branch literally had the keys to all our houses.

Richard reads out the statement made by the Metropolitan Police in response to my claim, served on them earlier today by my lawyers. Assistant Commissioner Martin Hewitt, who made the groundbreaking apology to the other women just two months ago, says that the Metropolitan Police no longer sanctioned: 'Long term deployments into protest groups but would accept responsibility for past failures, especially because there was a risk of collateral intrusion.'

Collateral intrusion. That is how they are describing me. I am fascinated. This feels like a scientific experiment. I wonder what they called me before, when they were scoping me out to be duped by Carlo. Was I a target? I wonder what notes they collated on my appearance, my character, my sexual preferences, my family history, my past mental health problems. I wonder if they know I had an abortion at twenty-one, even though I was in a long-term relationship. Would there be a note on my boyfriend, The Artist? Would they mention that the morning-after pill failed? I had briefly considered keeping the baby, but he and my mum were adamant that it was a crazy idea. Would they discuss the most intimate parts of my life in their safe houses, the half-way houses where they met in groups of five or six, each operative deployed into a different activist group? Would they share lewd stories, compare the breast sizes of the women they were sleeping with? I shudder at the thought of my secrets laid bare.

As the *Newsnight* credits roll, my phone starts to vibrate furiously again. Message after message, congratulating me on how calm I am, how dignified. My mum, sister, uncle. Old friends from Scotland: Kirsty, Rowan, Paula, Tania. The activist group: Helen, Alison, Harriet, Kate, Dan, Steve, Den, Paul. But the one that makes me laugh is from Dave Smith:

Anonymity my arse . . . anyone can tell it's you from your green nails! Well done, comrade xx

My trademark dark-green nails are now immortalised on screen. Not my face though. It is a surreal experience.

The adrenalin dissipates and I sleep easily, somehow. But the next day, I am bombarded with phone calls and requests for interviews. No, I just can't do it, not today, I tell Harriet, who is fielding the calls. Alison and Helen tell me not to worry, they will sort it out. Someone else can go on Radio 4 today and comment on the undercover policing scandal. I've had enough exposure on the BBC for one week.

I need to mentally recover, do something mundane and normal. I get heightened with the highs of this whole theatre and I get flattened by the lows. I am proud of myself and the film, yet at the same time I feel as though someone has ripped me open and exposed my innards to the world.

I am being dissected again and again and I am willingly consenting to it. I wonder if I gain something from the pain. A small part of me asks if I deserve it, but I push that voice away, using all my training, all my knowledge of the human mind. That morning I put my phone down, my laptop in the desk drawer. I find the girls playing in the garden and tell them that we're going on an adventure to London. They shriek excitedly, rush to pack matching small bags with important toys, hats, gloves and sweets. I want to get out of here, jump on a train and find myself somewhere else.

We spend the day at the Science Museum, an adventure for small children, the entry price worth it to see the girls' delight as they experiment with sound and light machines. We stop exploring and pause for lunch, whatever they want, and we talk about everything interesting to little girls. I realise they've grown up in these three months, have made some different friends at school, developed new passions. But I am reassured to see that they are happy, content.

I let the day stretch on, roasted chestnuts from a vendor outside, a London souvenir each from a garish gift shop before we catch the train home. I don't want to go back to the phone and everything it means. The next few weeks are going to be tough; Harriet has prepared me. There will be the response to our claim letter, the comments under the *Guardian* article to face, the public response to my personal life.

9

Neither Confirm nor Deny

Harriet calls me early on a hot July morning. She needs to tell me in advance that the Undercover Policing Inquiry will be publishing a document later today. Carlo has launched an application for an anonymity order to prevent his real name being published. He is already referred to within the public inquiry by his cypher, N104. All of the undercover spies have a number. It is confusing, trying to work out who is who.

The document I have been sent is heavily redacted. Blacked out, line after line. Do these covered-up words include my name, perhaps a description of my physical appearance? My health, my weaknesses, my vulnerabilities? What is it that Carlo is saying about me? The level of secrecy is unnerving. They can tell any old lies about me, but I cannot counter what I can't see.

It says he was deployed into extreme left-wing groups. This did not sound much like our life together, made up of social events, dinners and holidays. We went on a few counter-demonstrations together, against the BNP. Am I labelled an extremist for this? I laugh bitterly at the thought of it. They are just making things up. I know better than anyone that making things up works, especially when the victims are people the press and public like to point the finger at.

I'd told a colleague about my experience, and in the weeks following it had seen a drop in my freelance work. Was I being paranoid, or did they view me as a danger to their reputation? *There's no smoke without fire.* I print the document out and go through it line by line, trying to make sense of it, selecting the most important excerpts.

IN THE MATTER OF THE PUBLIC INQUIRY INTO UNDERCOVER POLICING OPEN APPLICATION ON BEHALF OF N104 FOR RESTRICTION ORDERS

5. *N104 was deployed to infiltrate extreme left-wing groups* **REDACTED** *and anti-fascist groups, including Anti-Fascist Action and No Platform. His/her deployment commenced in 2000 and concluded in 2006.*

6. **REDACTED** *N104 has neither self-disclosed nor been officially confirmed by the MPS or any other relevant body or court as being an undercover police officer. The degree of intrusion into N104's life* **REDACTED THREE LINES** *and has been highly intrusive.*

15. *N104 submits that Article 8 is engaged in his/her case. Refusal of the restriction orders applied for and the subsequent disclosure of N104's identity would undoubtedly result in an interference with him/her and his/her family's right to a private life.*

22. *Any public acknowledgement of N104's true identity would also have a serious and adverse effect on other close family members and potentially their reputation and professional lives and businesses.*

*(Followed by **eleven** fully redacted lines.)*

32. *It is on the basis that such assurances of confidence that N104 and other SDS undercover officers carried out their challenging and, on occasion, hazardous duties. It is also the basis upon which they organised their private and family lives. In his/her personal statement N104 records, prior to me accepting my deployment as an undercover officer I was given assurances by my employers that my identity would at all times remain confidential and that my role as a covert officer would never be confirmed or denied. I was assured that I would only ever be expected to provide intelligence and that nothing would ever be done that might risk me being exposed either in my covert identity or my real name. I relied on these assurances as did my then partner before I accepted this role.*

The document states that the undercover officers and their wives were given assurances that their identity would remain confidential, forever, ad infinitum. Their privacy must be protected. Their right to family life is enshrined in human rights law. Was this regardless of the crimes they committed? They committed miscarriages of justice and they instigated human rights abuses. What about my privacy and my right to family life? My head feels like it might explode. My body was used against my will. I did not consent to being a sexual experiment. I did not consent to being a mistress. I did not consent to being fucked all over the world by a man who did not exist. It seems they can act with impunity.

I watched *The Lives of Others* last night, spending most of the film crying inconsolably. It was my second time, having seen it when it was released back in 2006. I had thought it was a brilliant, artful film. Now I feel it is brilliant, artful and deeply sinister. It feels personal. I am obsessed by the lead female character, a beautiful, successful East German actress who is in a relationship with a well-known playwright. They are placed under surveillance and their flat is wiretapped because the playwright is suspected of writing for a West German newspaper. The Minister of Culture is obsessed with the actress too, and blackmails her into having sex with him. She cannot live with the shame and tragically dies by suicide.

I wonder what bothers me the most. Is it the physical intrusion that was carried out, the state-sanctioned misuse of sex? Or is it their knowledge of the very worst of me, the most unpleasant events in my life packaged into a small-town horror story? I remember all the things I told him. Our emotional intimacy, our shared language. The familiarity of dysfunction. I experience a kind of directionless rage that needs a home somewhere else, somewhere outside of my body.

'This is just like the Stasi,' I mutter to myself, slamming my laptop shut. I must get ready for another trip to London, but now I'm weary, my head achingly heavy. I feel like I'm carrying a stone-cold weight in my heart.

Lisa, the activist with the mellifluous Welsh voice, has Ricky Tomlinson in tears. They are on a stage together at SOAS, a department of the University of London, giving a talk on the impact of undercover policing. The audience is a sea of familiar faces: activists, famous trade unionists I know from the telly, the women, the socialists, the builders. Harriet, of course, our lawyer. Some anarchists I have not seen before. Journalists, including Rob Evans and Conrad Landin, a tall guy from the *Morning Star*.

Lisa tells her story, about her six-year relationship with Mark Kennedy, the most well known of the spycops. His photos are very much in the public domain. Lisa unmasked him back in

2011, and in doing so broke the story in the mainstream press. It dominated the front pages and led to tabloid reporters camping out at her door. At the end of Lisa's talk, Ricky Tomlinson hugs her, and his voice cracks as he takes the microphone to talk about his own experience.

Ricky is a successful comedy actor and he is also one of the Shrewsbury 24, a group of striking building workers who were charged with multiple public order offences following the first ever national building workers' strike in 1972. Twenty-four were charged with over 242 offences between them, including unlawful assembly, affray, intimidation, criminal damage and assault. They were prosecuted in 1973. Tomlinson and Des Warren were jailed, for two and three years respectively. In prison they were punished with solitary confinement and visits from family were blocked. Tomlinson served all except four months of his sentence. After their release from jail, they were blacklisted, notorious among employers.

Des Warren developed symptoms in prison similar to the Parkinson's disease that was to confine him to a wheelchair for the final five years of his life; he blamed his health problems on the tranquilliser drugs administered to difficult prisoners, the so-called 'liquid cosh'.

Tomlinson believes that there was collusion between the government, the police and the building trade to create the charges, to make an example of the strikers. Shrewsbury was a huge miscarriage of justice, which Ricky has always maintained resulted in his friend Des Warren's premature death.

As I sit in the audience surrounded by my new friends, many of whom were also targets of police abuse, I am acutely aware of how deep the wounds are, and how the absence of truth and justice means the healing hasn't even begun.

*   *   *

In the student bar afterwards, abuzz with people, I spot Lois from the Socialist Party. We had met up a few months before, in the stuffy, yellow-walled RMT office in Dover port. I had listened to her do a talk on spycops and then we had walked together to the train station, squeezing in a half-pint in the pub opposite before our train arrived. Lois was heading back to London; I had one stop to Folkestone. We spent that hurried drink in the pub reminiscing about our past lives, sharing what we knew about Carlo.

Lois and I had actually met some twelve years before at a Women's Day event. She had been a friend of Tania's. It was strange to think that we had been connected all this time, unwittingly. I knew Lois before I met the activists, before I met the women, before I met Harriet, before I met Rob, before the story went live. Lois and I had not seen each other in over a decade. This was another strange reunion sparked by the spy in our midst. Lois, an activist since she was a teenager, had been spied on not just by Carlo, but also by Peter Francis, the undercover officer who became a whistle-blower.

As soon as she sees me she comes over. 'Donna – you look totally different!'

'Oh my God, Lois! I've lost a stone since I saw you in Dover!' I twirl around, lifting my tartan shirt above my waist to show off my size-12 jeans. 'Bloody stress of all this has made me sick!'

I've been struggling with my autoimmune condition since 2012, but it was particularly angry around the time of the RMT meeting. I was desperately trying to keep things together, between work and the kids and the legal case. My body eventually gave in to the onslaught of symptoms, and I had a flare-up that led to pleurisy and kept me housebound for three weeks.

'I'm so sorry I didn't come last week, we had family stuff . . . I heard your talk was great,' she says, hand on my arm.

I had spoken publicly for the first time at a conference on blacklisting, organised by Dave Smith and the Blacklist Support Group. I could not remember a time when I'd been so anxious. My hands were shaking so much that I couldn't lift a glass of water and so my mouth got drier and drier, to the point where it seemed I might choke. Yet, at the same time, this unnerving experience felt cathartic. At the end, something had shifted in me. I felt stronger, more connected to the activists around me. I felt a huge sense of belonging.

'I was utterly petrified,' I confess to Lois now, 'but I wanted this out in the world. Did you notice the perfect timing? Conrad's story on the very front page of the *Morning Star*?'

Conrad Landin has an interest in politics, corruption and trains. He consistently turns up at every spycop event and I've got to know him a little. We have a shared love of Glasgow, Marseille and French crime fiction. Conrad's story told how Carlo had tried to incite some of the activists to firebomb a charity shop, which he'd told us had links to the Armed Revolutionary Nuclei, an Italian fascist group. They were believed to be responsible for the Bologna train station bombing.

Conrad had spoken to the activists, who had decided to expose the story. How Carlo had insisted on the role the charity shop owner had played, pressing the other men on their commitment to the cause. The story was plastered over the front page, Carlo looking suitably sinister, the headline reading:

Spycop told activists to BURN charity

I had used the newspaper as a convenient prop when I spoke in public that first time, holding up Carlo's best sinister photo to the open-mouthed audience, barely able to disguise my trembling hands. I had read the article online, on the train into London. I cornered Conrad as soon as I arrived, relieved he was there and eager to see if he had a print copy of the paper. He had gone scouting around all of Greenwich until he found a newsagent that sold the *Morning Star.*

The image of Carlo on the front page of the newspaper was powerful: a striking monochrome portrait, the trademark designer sunglasses shielding his eyes. Goatee beard neatly trimmed. No smile.

He could pass for either mafiosi or *carabinieri*. There wasn't a hair's breadth between them.

The bar becomes quieter, people leaving in ones and twos to jump on the bus or catch the tube back to the outer zones of London. There is only a handful of us left. Me, Helen, Harriet, Aidan, a couple of the builders.

'Watch the time!' Helen gestures at her watch; in the few months since I've known her, I've already had several last-train near-misses. I was always last to leave the party, but now that I live on the coast the night bus option is gone.

'One more and then I promise I'll go! It's my turn to get a round in.'

Rules for living: always buy your round, wear SPF every day and never cross a picket line.

As I stand waiting for my drinks to be poured, I feel eyes on me. Standing at the other end of the bar is a younger man, in his early thirties. Tall and quite stocky, wearing an Aran knit jumper and a Barbour-type waxed jacket. He doesn't smile when I meet his gaze, which I find odd, and I can't work out who he is with. Not the socialists or the builders. He doesn't particularly look like one of the anarchists.

I take my change and carry the last drinks of the evening back to my table. 'Do you know him?' I nudge Harriet, gesturing over to the still-staring man. 'Have you seen him before?'

'No, I don't think so,' she says, shaking her head, turning back to her conversation with Helen.

Maybe he is a lawyer or a journalist, but it seems unlikely. He has started talking to a group of students. I keep half an eye on him but get distracted by one of Helen's stories. Next time I look up he is gone.

'Right, madam! Time to get going!' Helen reminds me that I will absolutely miss the last train home if I don't leave right now.

'Shit!' I grab my rucksack. 'Love you all!'

I blow kisses to the small assembly of the country's most respected activists, who are posing for a photo in the hallway, and run down the stairs, almost tripping over myself.

As I hit the cool of the night air, my eyes adjust to the darkness, and I'm suddenly aware of the time and also that I have no bearings whatsoever. Fuck. Which way is King's Cross? I start walking straight ahead, rooting around in my rucksack, trying to locate my phone to look at the map, becoming annoyed with myself. If I miss this train, I'll be stranded in London. I can always sleep on a sofa, but I have work in the morning in Dover.

To my left, a sudden movement catches my eye. Turning my head, I realise it is him, the man in the waxed jacket from the bar upstairs. The hairs on my neck go up and a rush of anxiety explodes in my gut. Has he been waiting for me all along? I have to make a decision – go back inside to the others or keep walking. I must go home, work tomorrow. I quicken my steps. Behind me, the footsteps become louder, closer. He is definitely following me. I'm lost, my breathing is shallow and my brain is starting to fog with fear.

I turn to look at him and he stops dead, stares right at me with cold eyes, then moves off to the side, now walking in parallel with me. This is a game. I can see a turn-off approaching, a more brightly lit street. I gulp in some air and keep going, hoping for people, traffic, something safe.

Suddenly, a hundred metres ahead, I spot a familiar figure. Liam. Relief. I can tell it is him from his gait and his short, muscular frame. I remember saying goodbye to him moments before. I yell his name, willing my fear-shrivelled voice to find its shape again. 'Liam!'

He doesn't hear me and the footsteps quicken beside me, closer again, more hurried.

'LIAM!'

This time my voice elevates above the dark streets, catching Liam just before he turns the corner. He stops and looks back at me in surprise.

'Wait!' I wave furiously. 'Wait for me!'

Liam starts walking back towards me. I catch waxed-jacket man slipping off to the side, into the private residents' garden.

'Oh my God, Liam, I'm so glad to see you!' I point to the gated gardens. 'Someone was following me. He's just gone in there.'

We both catch a final glimpse of the sinister figure as he disappears among the rose bushes.

'Fuckin' hell, D! Where are you going?'

'King's Cross – St Pancras I mean. Last train.' I am shaking now, and can hardly form a sentence.

'Come on.' He gently takes my elbow. 'I'll walk with you. Who is he?'

'I don't know. I've never seen him before tonight, but he was definitely in the bar earlier. He was really staring at me. I asked, but no one seemed to know him.'

'Special Branch. I'll bet my life.'

'You mean an undercover cop?' I am incredulous.

'Yep, I'd hazard a guess that he's one of Carlo's mates. Probably designed to freak you out. He wasn't spying on you, Donna. He wanted you to see him.'

'Why? Why would they do this now?'

'Because you spoke in public last week. You're being interviewed in the papers. You've stuck your head right above the parapet, that's why. They're trying to intimidate you.'

Liam walks me all the way to the ticket barrier and insists on waiting until I am safely on the train.

The journey home is deeply unsettling. I eye everyone with suspicion. The drunk businessman singing to himself in the corner, is he pretending to be inebriated? The homeless guy with the rucksack, is he a state actor too? The blonde woman who is slumped with her head on the table, short leopard-print dress, clutching a garishly embellished bag. Is she really asleep? I'm on hyper-alert for the fifty-minute journey.

Finally, the hellish journey is almost over and we approach Folkestone. I stand up, scanning the carriage to see who is getting off at this station. I rush off the train as soon as the doors open, running up the walkway to get myself out of the empty, ghostly station. The sky is indigo, the streetlights so dimmed that they are useless to me. I now have a shadowy walk under the railway bridge and then a few minutes skirting alongside the vast unlit park to get myself home safely. The night is silent. Not even a scavenging fox in sight to offer me some company.

I finally get my key to turn in the lock and stumble into the hallway. The dogs begin barking furiously, unsettled. I throw my rucksack down and drop to the floor beside them, reaching out for comfort, sobbing in uncontrolled waves.

I have always loved the night; a fear of the shadows is not something I had bargained for among the rest of this madness.

10

What Is True?

Carlo: Locksmith/Activist/Fiancé.
Carlo: Spycop/State-sponsored liar/Someone else's husband.

It's late 2017 and I'm writing down the history of my relationship with Carlo on giant Post-it notes, remembering the key events as best I can. This is in preparation for making a police complaint, which is a legal challenge in addition to the civil case I launched in January 2016. As my relationship began after the Human Rights Act came into force in 2000 there are several legal options open to me. The question is how much do I want to fight, and how much fight do I have in me?

I keep returning to the Bologna trip in February 2003. I talked about it for months afterwards. Years even. Long after Carlo had disappeared. Planning a holiday with my sister, I suggest we go to Italy.

'You would love Bologna. We can go to the Diana restaurant, the posh one.'

'Didn't you go there with Carlo? Won't going back upset you?'

'Oh God no, not after all these years. Bologna is beautiful. Why should I let him ruin it for me?' I knew it would hurt though, retracing those steps. Those sites of incredible love and passion.

*　　*　　*

The Diana was one of the classic Emilian restaurants. Not great for vegetarians, but I still ate meat back then. It was Carlo's favourite restaurant, or so he said. He had booked a table. It was so popular you had to book weeks in advance. Before we went, we had several Rossinis, which we drank headily in a socialist bar decked out in red from floor to ceiling, close to the Due Torri. Carlo made me go to the bar to practise my Italian, which was non-existent. I could say, '*Ti amo pui de calcio,*' and that was it.

He planned every moment of the trip, booked the flights and the hotel and filled our days with a roster of Bologna's best sites. Museums, yes, but also beautiful streets, quiet bars, big events. He had booked us tickets to see Bologna play football. I had never been to a match in Europe and it was a revelation. Armed police, dogs, flares going off everywhere. It was cold and he wrapped himself around me to keep me warm, extracting himself only when Bologna scored.

I love you more than football. He said this to me every day, his working-man mantra, though the last part was interchangeable. More than words. More than the sunset over the Isle of Arran. I love you more than wine. More than money. More than the stars up in the sky. Every day. I can't remember if I had a mantra for him too. I remember feelings more than words; images, physical sensations.

We stayed in a five-star hotel and Carlo insisted on ordering room service at breakfast each day. I had never had room service before. I laughed and teased him as they wheeled in the cart, plates piled high. 'Bloody champagne socialist, you are!' We had left plenty of time in the schedule to stay in bed.

On our way to Bologna, the heat and beauty enticed me, but more than that it was the chance to be close to him. To his roots.

I knew he'd spent so much time there, seeing family that extended out from the heart of the city.

I remember how disappointed I felt when he announced that we couldn't go and visit his dad, but he said he wanted this trip to be just for us, celebrating his birthday and Valentine's Day. No family or friends, just me and him. We would meet his father on the next trip – a longer one, he promised. He would introduce me to all the cousins, and the aunties who were still alive.

I write the words Not True Stories on one of the giant Post-it notes and stick it in the middle of the wall. Then start to recall:

1. VANESSA FELTZ

Carlo was a locksmith.

Carlo said he did some work for Vanessa Feltz. He described the opulent staircase in the centre of her north-London house, with a crystal chandelier hanging above, and a huge portrait of Vanessa wearing a flouncy pink dress hanging on the wall.

Ostentatious, he called it.

Recently one of the women did an interview with Vanessa Feltz. I wished it had been me, just so I could tell her about Carlo and ask if she really had a giant portrait of herself on the top landing and a crystal chandelier above the staircase. Just imagine if she'd said yes.

2. THE JESUS AND MARY CHAIN

We were on the London Underground on a Saturday night. I remember changing lines at Oxford Circus, from the Bakerloo onto the Victoria line. We were heading south to Stockwell. It was a Saturday night, and we had been invited to a comrade's birthday party. There must have been a gig on at the Brixton Academy, judging by the swarm of Jesus and Mary Chain T-shirts.

'You must like the Jesus and Mary Chain,' Carlo had said, 'being Scottish?'

'Never really listened to them. Do you?'

'Love them. "April Skies" is one of my favourite songs . . .'

I already have Spotify playing from my phone. I change the song. 'April Skies' bursts out of my Bose speaker. I write down the lyrics on one of the giant notes:

> *Baby baby, I just can't see*
> *Just what you mean to me*
> *I take my aim and I fake my words*
> *I'm just your long-time curse . . .'*

3. ILA

'Ila says hi!' Carlo turned his head slightly, so he could see me, cupping his hand over the phone. He winked.

'Love right back at her!'

'Donna sends love. She's just in from work. She's had a tough week.'

I heard her voice, distant on the other end of the phone. I mouthed at him, I love you, as I left the room. One of our clients had died the previous day, from an oesophageal bleed. He was a long-term drinker, an Irish man from Derry. I knew him from when I lived in the squat in Vauxhall. We drank in the same pub, where they served the best Guinness in London. Carlo had held me tightly when I cried in bed.

Ila was Carlo's older sister. We'd never met. She lived in

Peterborough, which she hated, and was stuck in a deeply unhappy marriage. She felt trapped, she was depressed, and she spent her days drinking tea and smoking in the kitchen. She didn't like visitors. No wonder, I thought. It all sounded grim. Especially Peterborough. Carlo didn't paint a flattering picture of the town. 'You will get to meet her soon,' he promised me. He drove up there once or twice a month to see her. She very rarely went out. They spoke on the phone at least twice a week.

I remember my empathy for this fake Ila. The real Ila wasn't depressed at all. She had a successful business and a handsome husband and a beautiful house. I'd found this out on Facebook. It wasn't Ila he spoke to twice a week on the phone, who I shouted hi to. It was a woman, but not his sister. Certainly not his wife. Who was she?

I know deep down who she had to be. I write it on the Post-it note in spiky black letters:

LIES   POLICE HANDLER

4. Anne

Carlo told me he met Anne, his son's mother, when he did some work on her parents' home. They owned a big house in a civilised north-London suburb. He said she was a journalist, that she was older than him and it was a fling that lasted only a few weeks. She got pregnant and wanted the baby but not him. He said she was quite difficult, aloof, posh. Made it hard for him to see the baby, so in the end he gave up. He'd told me this fairly early on, in some version of a 'cards on the table' talk to start our relationship on an honest footing. He didn't want to say much though, only that he missed his son, hardly saw him.

She got in touch a few months into our relationship though, wanted him to get involved. She didn't want money, but she wanted help with childcare as she had moved to Cornwall and needed to make regular trips back to London for work. She wanted him to stay in her house, to take care of the boy in Cornwall when she travelled.

'Can't she bring Freddie here, Carlo? We can look after him in London, if she's coming up anyway?'

'She won't let you meet him yet, darlin'. She wants to wait until she knows it's solid between us. Doesn't want different women in and out of his life.'

'Of course we're bloody solid! We're getting married for God's sake!'

'I know, I know, my darlin', but she's a bit difficult. And protective of Freddie. That's understandable. She's used to having all the responsibility for him. It's me she doesn't trust yet, not you. She thinks I'm unreliable.'

'She's the one who messed you around though! You said you had wanted to see him and she kept putting barriers in your way.'

'I know. I know it's not fair. But I want to build a relationship with Freddie. He's going to be a big part of our life. Let's just take it slowly with Anne. Please, Donna, be patient.'

After that he started disappearing off every other week, down to Cornwall for the weekend. When he came back he'd show me photos of the boy, playing on the beach or running in front of him. He glowed with pride, and I'd suggest again that I go with them. He always said no, and I'd be left asking myself what hold this woman, Anne, had over him.

*   *   *

On my final Post-it note I write WIFE and add it to my installation of lies.

I look up at the wall of deceit, bright pinks and yellows drawing my eye to the lies that dictated my life. I can't bear to look at it any more; I leave the room and shut the door behind me. I'll come back to it.

11

Disintegration

No one seems interested when I tell them about being followed by the stranger in the waxed jacket. They acknowledge it, briefly, then quickly move the conversation on. It feels like they really do not want to know. Or maybe they think I am becoming obsessive? I keep on repeating the story, to different people, testing for a different reaction. This is fruitless. How can they all dismiss something so serious, so sinister? I want some acknowledgement, some recognition of what's happening.

Throughout that winter and into the endless months of 2017 I seek out old acquaintances, people I haven't seen in a long time, to tell them what really happened with Carlo. People who actually knew him back then, who ate his risottos and his *pasta in brodo* and laughed at his Elvis impersonations. I am working in London for a few days, and meet up with old, familiar faces in the pub every night, desperately trawling through the contacts in my phone like an addict in need of a hit. Lucy, Katie, Mike. We all know each other from our time working in homelessness services, but I meet up with them individually, expanding my night-out options. They all knew Carlo, as he was happy to come on nights out with the work crowd.

Lucy and I arrange to meet in Bradley's Spanish Bar. It is a ferociously hot, packed pub close to where we emerge from the bowels of London at Tottenham Court Road. We remember a night out there with Carlo. He came straight from work, sweating furiously in a grey hoodie. He took it off, lifting up a faded red anti-fascist T-shirt to show a muscular, hairy torso. Lucy had raised an eyebrow at me. She was quite merry. We were on our third glass.

'Do you remember the Elvis funeral story, lass?'

'Hang on, doll. I've just put this on the jukebox!'

Elvis came on. 'Suspicious Minds'.

Carlo started miming along, a rolled-up crisp packet becoming a microphone in his hand, exaggerating his facial movements like a *Spitting Image* puppet.

'Did you listen to Elvis much in Italy, Carlo?' Lucy smiled wryly, sniffing her Rioja, which was a bit on the vinegary side. 'We loved him in Carlisle. And Scotland too, eh doll?' She nodded to me.

'Elvis was King in Modena!!! Did I ever tell you, ladies, I want an Elvis funeral?'

He turned to face me.

'Seriously, darlin' – I want to go out in style. Dressed in a white suit with flares and a big collar, with my coffin in the sidecar of a motorbike.'

Lucy laughed again. 'Where did you find this eejit, Donna?'

'I felt sorry for him, doll. He was loitering by some railings at St James's Park, looking lost and lonesome.' I played along.

Carlo pulled me into his body, wrapping his big arm around my front.

'Look at her now!' he gestured to me. 'After all this, and she's agreed to marry me! She must be as crazy as I am!'

One evening I'm sitting across from Mike, who used to be a frequent guest at our table, often the last one there, talking into

146

the night with Carlo. I can't bring myself to tell Mike that I suspect Carlo was involved in a miscarriage of justice that affected him directly. It took years for him to get over the homophobic assault that happened in Brixton, outside the Ritzy. The witnesses retracted their statements, the CCTV went missing.

The attack had happened not long before I left Steve's (which had been short-term) and moved in with Matt – who had witnessed the assault – after Carlo left. When Carlo came back into my life, after that evening with the expensive meal, he spent nights with me at Matt's flat. The police investigating the assault had intimidated Mike and Matt to drop the case and had used private information to do so. Matt believed his phone was being tapped. We were sure the perpetrator was a police informant, and that was why they wanted the case dropped. Now I know that Carlo could have been feeding information to his mates, the investigating officers, and it weighs heavily on me. I feel like I've personally let Mike down. Guilt and shame are unpleasant company.

I explain all this to Mike, topping up our glasses as I pour my heart out. He listens gravely, then reaches his hands across to mine. We've been friends for nearly two decades, before Carlo and after him. His forgiveness makes me weep and we end up talking into the night.

Weeks go by in a blur of too much alcohol and too many hangovers. I under-sleep and overspend, buying unnecessary gifts for the children and expensive face cream for myself, hoping it might mitigate against the lack of sleep and dehydration. Behaving recklessly and impulsively, I feel that I am losing the very core of my being. This could be 2004 all over again. Or 1986.

My exterior somehow remains intact, polished even. An expensive coat can hide a multitude of vulnerabilities. I had realised this in my teens, when I saved up my earnings from the Taj to buy expensive perfume and sleek black clothes. I'm sure my granny told me something similar, about the coat, but she hadn't owned an expensive item of clothing in her life.

To the group, I'm powering through, resilient and strong. We are busy all the time, all working round the clock to push forward the case, to draw attention to the inquiry and raise public awareness of the extent of the undercover policing scandal. I am speaking at big events on a regular basis. I've come to realise that speaking is a tool of activism, an important way of taking action. I'm told that I am confident and natural as a public speaker. This masks my inner deconstruction of myself into a million fragmented pieces. I wonder if I can put myself back together again.

As well as facilitating the mental health groups, I also work freelance, training groups of healthcare workers around the country in treatment models for behavioural change. I fly by the seat of my pants, relying on caffeine, strong words and quick thoughts to get through each day. I am frequently underprepared, leaving everything until the last minute. My residual energy is focused on meeting up with people I vaguely knew in the past or chatting to complete strangers. I like being in hotels, away from my domestic life. I am struggling to be fully present with the kids, emotionally. A hungover mum on autopilot. I can't read a book or fully concentrate on a film. My mind drifts, replaying past scenes of failure, of vulnerability. This is a form of self-punishment. I flit between tasks, writing a single page of a report, jumping to answering emails, then scanning an unrelated document, leaving bits of discarded paper to waft to the floor. I exist in barely managed chaos.

'Have you thought about counselling?' Alison sits close beside me in the busy hotel bar. I'm due to catch my train home from St Pancras to the seaside after a few days in London when she happens to call. She is nearby, just finishing a meeting at the British Library.

'Shall we catch up for half an hour?'

'Yes, let's meet in the hotel bar, the one next to King's Cross station.'

I'm grateful that my time in London is extended for a while.

It's becoming very gentrified around King's Cross. The hotel is newly refurbished, and a cup of tea is the price of a pint anywhere else. I worked around this area years ago, supporting young homeless Scots. Most had come from abusive, neglectful backgrounds and had fled south to escape. I guess I had fled several times too, in my own way. I feel like fleeing again.

Alison pours milk into her china cup of extra-strong tea, while I cradle a glass of Sauvignon Blanc.

'Counselling? No way. The last counsellor I saw told me I was too fucked up to deal with. She was shit. She signed me up for twelve sessions and then dumped me on the second one.'

'What did you do, threaten to kill her? "I'll murder you if you write bad things about me." '

Alison peers at me over her glasses, giggling at her terrible Scottish accent.

'What?! I only told her I'd had an eating disorder when I was young, and I had issues with relationships.'

We laugh. Alison understands. I don't need to explain any further. She believes me about the strange man who followed me, as does Helen. They told me similar things had happened to them after they found out about their ex-partners. Sinister things.

'I feel on edge, constantly anxious. Like there's someone just hovering behind me, out of sight.' My eyes dart around the bar, which is bloated with red-faced, thick-necked businessmen. Men in suits. Any of them could be undercover, monitoring us and recording our interactions.

'It's hardly surprising, is it? This is a normal response to an abnormal situation.' Alison sips her tea.

'Has anyone looked at that?' I wonder aloud. 'From a research perspective, I mean. What happens when a group of people find out a big chunk of their life was a total deception?'

'We've thought about speaking to a psychologist, to look at funding a study into the trauma. And about doing a documentary. It's so hard though. People get sick of living it every day. They don't want to go over and over and over it.' She pulls at a tuft of her hair, a little habit I've noticed before. An unconscious coping mechanism. 'And the other thing is, the psychiatric assessments are gruesome! You know that – you've experienced it. It drills into every aspect of your life, touching all the nerves. Didn't you find that when you saw whatsherface?'

'Dr Clifton? I liked her. But it unlocked so many old doors. The whole fucking contents of the attic came flying out at once, sharp objects wounding me as they hit. It's not normal, having to expose your entire life story to a complete stranger in one sitting. A stranger who also has all of your medical records in front of them!' I pause to gulp some wine. 'If you went to see a therapist in the real world, you would at least have the safety of revealing things bit by bit. Or not at all if it was too raw. This process is brutal, like having someone operate on you without an anaesthetic.'

We form a bond of silence together for a few moments, amidst the conversations and the clatter of the bar. It crosses my mind that the process of holding the police to account is designed to be as painful as possible. First, they invade your body, then your mind, and finally your entire life. Then years later, when you uncover the truth, they do it all over again.

Violation after violation.

2018

Dr Clifton had opened the heavy, ornate door to a Georgian building just off High Holborn. She was clear-skinned, with a measured smile, expensive clothes put together in a simple but stylish ensemble. Everything about her was the opposite of me. I had been outside in the traffic-laden street for five minutes, trying to work out which buzzer to press, spilling hot black coffee down the front of my best coat as I leaned in to see the tiny writing on the intercom.

'We're on the first floor. Do you want to walk or take the lift?'

'Walking is fine, thanks.' Sniffing my coat sleeve as I walked behind her. I smelled like a Costa coffee shop.

'Shall I come with you?' Helen had phoned to ask.

'Or meet you afterwards?' Alison rang me as well.

She's been on the phone to Helen, I thought, *talking about me.*

'Dear God, no. I'll be fine, don't worry!'

It will be gruesome, Alison and Helen had warned; the psych assessments required for their legal case had been tough. Even

Harriet said I should prepare myself for some emotional fallout.

Dr Clifton had my medical notes in front of her. They were huge.

'This should take about two hours,' she said.

We were there for almost three. I didn't think I would cry. I convinced myself it was going to be straightforward. The dainty box of tissues in front of me had to be replenished, I went through so many of them.

She had asked me how Carlo managed to form such a close emotional bond with me so quickly.

'What was it that connected you?'

'Domestic abuse. His father was violent. So was mine.'

I'll tell you my darkness if you tell me yours.

Prestwick, 1981

'Just call me angel of the morning . . . *ANGEL!*'

Emphatic high pitch on the second 'angel'. The damn ironing song, my mum performing along to the radio as she pressed the whites down on the faded orange board with the iron. I hated the hot sizzle, that smell on the much-washed cotton school shirts. We had no money but *jeeso*, we were clean. Hoover, iron, bleach. The smells and sounds of a well-kept house. A mad house, but no midden. Sunday evenings were built for tension in our small house, heightened by the burning smell of the iron and the soaring vocals of 'Angel of the Morning'. There was a hair-trigger tension in the air. Mum sang her way through it. I bit my nails and tapped my fingers.

'Donna, you're an awful fidget,' tutted my gran.

I chewed the ends off pencils and doodled constantly. Couldn't sit still.

Sundays were prime pub afternoons for my father. Dinner would be ready at five – usually a gammon joint, hotpot or mince and tatties, always with diced carrots. He rarely made it home before eight. To distract myself I often watched the black-and-white telly, which sat in the corner of the room on a teak unit with silver photo frames positioned carefully at each side. Me and my sister in summer frocks; my sister in her Silver Cross pram with a big smile, blonde curls spilling out from under a white woolly bonnet, me peeking in to tickle her, the side of my face visible. Dark hair, dark eyes, pale skin.

On this day the TV programme was about mute teenage twin girls who became arsonists and ended up in a place that was both a hospital and a prison, a 'secure unit'. They weren't medically mute, they just wouldn't speak to anyone, only communicated to each other in a non-verbal language. Of course it went unsaid, but we were on edge, brittle, waiting for him to get in. Wondering what the state of him would be tonight.

This particular evening, I was more anxious than usual. Tensions had been building before he even left for the Red Lion. It must have been winter because it was already dark and the new gas fire was on full blast, suffocating me. The council had started a new programme of modernisation, putting in central heating and gas fires in all the houses on the estate. We had to move out for three weeks and stayed just around the corner in Sanquhar Avenue, with my granny. I loved staying with my gran. I would have lived there forever and not gone back to that bare-floored new house with the neighbour up the stairs, who played piano really loudly and shouted at us when we played in our own garden. She spied on us any time we were outside, waiting for what, I don't know.

The three weeks staying with Gran hadn't gone brilliantly though, as my dad found a reason to criticise her to my mother every day.

'Your mother is always interfering, Anne!'

'Interfering? Aye? She let us live here for five years and now she's letting us stay again!'

'Oh, fuck her . . . and you!'

The tension had continued when we came back to our own house, as the next step in the modernisation programme meant that my gran had to come and stay with us while her own gas fire and central heating were being installed by the council workmen. On this anxious night, watching the mute arsonist twins in Broadmoor, I knew that Gran would be arriving first thing in the morning, and still the clock ticked on with no sign of my father. His dinner was turning to carbon in the oven, the smell of overcooked gammon catching the back of my throat. I wanted to vomit. My stomach was heaving. I'd recently decided to stop eating meat, a decision that hadn't been well received by anyone, either at home or by the dinner ladies at school. I had free school meals, so had no choice but to queue every day for mash and meat. I'd starting asking for just the veg. There was a battle every day and the woman who supervised us eating was the scariest flame-haired, high-heeled tyrant I'd met. But at eight I was stubborn and I lacked both fear and an off switch.

'Just call me angel of the morning . . . *ANGEL*! Just touch my cheek before you leave me . . . baby!'

Feet heavily coming up the path. The door handle turning. The slowness of the steps and the movement of the lock were an indication of the level of inebriation. Too slow, deliberate. The air was thick.

The floorboards from the front door through the hallway

creaking. The incessant noise of the telly from the upstairs flat pounding down through the living-room ceiling. *Songs of Praise* or some other shite.

Footsteps straight into the kitchen. Over to the cooker. Oven door slamming open. The tray pulled out.

BANG.

Dinner on the floor: burnt gammon, smashed potatoes. The Pyrex dish in smithereens.

In he rages now, a sweating, clammy mass of pissed-up fury.

'Whit are you looking at? Get to yer bed, lady.'

'She hasn't had her ba—'

'Don't you fuckin' talk back to me!'

'Donna, go to your room!'

My mum by the ironing board still.

Locked in the bathroom, I sit down on the bare floor and lean my head against the new radiator. BANG. My head. Bang, bang, bang. Slowly and deliberately hitting my head. Screams. Hers or mine?

'Just call me angel of the morning . . . ANGEL! Just touch my cheek before you leave me . . . BABY!'

Why did this have to tap into my childhood? It was meant to be about Carlo.

Shrinks. It had been a while, but this wasn't the first time, nor would it be the last.

1988

I was going to walk to the hospital from the town centre, save the bus fare. Someone beeped their horn and then pulled over as I marched along the main road. I jumped, hyper-alert, and then realised it was Jim the painter. He was a regular at the Taj, at least thirty, and he was in love with me. I was sixteen.

'Where you off to, Donna? Do you want a lift?' he shouted from the window of his white Ford van.

'Oh, thanks, but I'm just going to the hospital up the road.' I pointed into the distance at the grey Victorian building, which was flanked by huge trees.

'You mean the weans' hospital?' He looked confused. Why would I, a woman in his eyes, be attending a children's hospital? 'Do you not want a lift?'

Deciding it would be simpler if I said yes, I opened the passenger door and climbed in. 'I've got an interview for a work placement. I might apply to do psychology.' Quick thinking, girl.

'I thought you were going to the art school?'

'Keeping my options open just now, Jim. I've been reading a bit of Freud and R.D. Laing.'

'Aye, fair enough,' he agreed. Didn't say much the rest of the journey, just glanced over at me every few seconds. As I walked away from his van I felt his eyes on me, but I never looked back.

I sat in the waiting room looking at the pink doll's house and the display of tattered picture books. I felt like an awkward giant. A small girl with messy hair and big dark circles under her eyes left the consulting room, staring at me and clutching her mother's hand. She kept on staring even as she was forced towards the exit, turning her wee head around for as long as she could. Even a mentally ill child could see right through me.

'Miss McLean?' I was swiftly summoned to Dr McKay's room. He was round. Very round. Bald, with a baby-pink head. Small glasses. Ruddy cheeks and nose. He gestured for me to come in. 'Please, take a seat.'

An armchair, worn but comfy. He sat behind a wooden desk but didn't make quite enough room for his plump thighs to fit underneath, so had to wheel his chair a fraction away from it.

'Miss McLean. May I call you Donna?'

'Yes, of course.' I nodded, folding my hands on my knees. 'Very nice to meet you.'

'So, we've had this referral from Dr . . . Hutcheson? Your family doctor, yes?'

He peered at me over his glasses. He didn't seem to have any eyebrows. He took a cigarette, Silk Cut, from a packet of ten that had been sitting on the desk beside a brown folder. My notes, I presumed. He lit and inhaled, then blew the smoke away from me.

'How are you feeling about being here today?'

I coughed. He was sitting in front of another doll's house. What was with all the doll's houses?

'Well.' I had decided in advance to be well spoken and composed, as I did not want an adverse diagnosis. I was not prepared to have a personality disorder. I'd looked it all up and realised it could go either way. 'Well . . . I'm pleased to be here. I think I may need some help with my mood.'

'Okay.' Dr McKay nodded slowly, appraising me. 'Describe your mood to me. Over the last couple of weeks, say?' He flicked his ash into a small green ceramic plate with black olives painted on it.

'My mood is very low. I have dark thoughts. I don't sleep much. I don't like being around people.' I'd decided in advance not to mention the self-induced vomiting or the self-mutilation. I wanted to test his expertise, see if he spotted these things for himself.

'Are you still managing to get to school, Donna?'

'Oh yes, I like being in the art department. No one bothers me there. Art helps.'

I didn't say I'd rather be anywhere than at home. The tension was unbearable. My dad was on long-term sick leave, still being paid, so he had enough money to go to the Red Lion every day. The week before he'd smashed the back-door window in a rage when I said he was rambling. At home we all existed in a state of brittle anticipation of the next flashpoint, the next threat. *Let's see if he works that out for himself too.*

'And friends? Do you have any close friends?'

'Well, my best friend, Lisa – we've been best friends since we were five – she's going to be a doctor so I don't see her as much these days. We met on the first day of primary one. She came up and asked me what was wrong with my teeth. Someone had dropped me face first on a sink you see, and all my front teeth had to come out in one go. At least they were only baby teeth.' I formed an exaggerated grin and pointed at my teeth. 'Anyway, Lisa's still my best friend, but she studies a lot.'

'Oh yes, of course, she must. Medicine is a hard road to choose, especially for a young woman.' He nodded, his chins bulging over a tight white shirt. His suit jacket was pale blue with an off-white stripe. It exhibited a cluster of egg-yolk stains down the front.

'And what will you do when you leave school? Have you thought about your plans?'

'Art school. I'm definitely going to art school.' It was the only answer I could come up with, though the thought terrified me. The art department was one thing – it was dark and safe – but a big art college filled with confident, middle-class, colourful people? I wasn't so sure about that.

'And is there a boyfriend on the scene yet?' He leaned towards me, his jacket straining at the shoulders. I could smell coffee breath.

'Well . . .' I paused for effect. 'That's really where it all went a bit wrong.'

'Where what went wrong?'

I explained about being a waitress and meeting Jas and how him being a Sikh meant it all went to pot once his family realised we were serious. And then we almost ran away to Birmingham and that really set the cat among the canaries.

'Quite dramatic then?' He appeared genuinely interested now. 'And you no longer work at this restaurant?'

'Well, actually, I am still there. His uncles – my bosses – sent him back to Wembley and they didn't sack me in the end. It's quite surprising really.'

'You must be a very good waitress, if they still want to hold onto you after all that trouble.'

'No, I'm a terrible waitress. I spilled a full bottle of house red on a customer's white linen suit just last week. Bobby – that's my boss – made me go and work in the kitchen until the woman left. She was really angry.'

Dr McKay nodded. He seemed quite understanding. I began to think that maybe this therapy business wouldn't be too bad.

It wasn't. I went for three months, chatted about my school life, my friends, my mum. At the end Dr McKay smiled down at me and said he thought I was doing very well. Best of luck.

2000

I wasn't in the abyss, so it wasn't like before, but I'd started having panic attacks again. Many years had passed since the last episode, and it unnerved me. The Artist and I were living in a one-room flat above a pub in Tooting, so he could have a separate studio space, up Garratt Lane, near the greyhound track.

Living above the pub became much too hectic, people ringing our buzzer as they went in, to ask if we would join them. Scottish lads, the art school crowd, the ex-soldier now a communications expert. He had an affectionate punch that left a small bruise. An eclectic mix. The screech of the buzzer went right through me, like tinfoil scraping. The tube journey to work had begun to unsettle me too. The creaking and shuddering of the train was inhabiting my own body. Something was on my back again. The noises too loud, the lights too bright, a sense of things lurking in the shadows. I had to keep my eyes shut.

I asked my GP if I could see a counsellor.

'I would advise medication,' he said. 'With your history . . .' He slowly thumbed through the heavy, well-worn brown file in front of him. It had a coffee stain on the front. Someone had put their sloppy cup down on my life story. Such a lot of notes, my life so far. I was only twenty-eight.

'Please – I'd like to give counselling a go. I'm having panic attacks and I feel claustrophobic in my flat, but I'm coping at work. I love work. I think I need to process some things from the past. I'd really prefer not to take drugs again.'

I convinced him with my reasoned argument. I saw the therapist for our first appointment a few weeks later.

We had our assessment and she said, 'Yes, I can work with you. Let's book twelve sessions. I'll call you to confirm a time.'

She rang me to arrange as promised. It was an efficient service.

'I'm looking forward to it,' I said, truthfully.

On the second appointment, she sat back stiffly in her chair, holding her papers like a shield. 'I've had second thoughts. I feel that you need more than counselling. I think you need long-term psychotherapy. I can suggest a few places if you would consider it? They offer low-cost options.'

I looked at the clock. We were five minutes into a fifty-minute session. She was dumping me. Stunned, I took the leaflets that she offered. She held them out gingerly, as if not to make contact with my skin.

On the humid tube train, hurtling north to work, I held the orange rail tightly and closed my eyes.

2005

The quirky French GP from my new Brixton surgery immediately agreed to send me to a psychologist.

'A psychologist, not a counsellor?'

'I think better in these circumstances, no?'

I agreed to give it a go.

A swift referral process and a few weeks later an assessment with Dr Berry, a chartered psychologist. I liked him. He was tanned and Antipodean, slickly dressed. No Vivien Leigh chat or bloody Rorschach or IQ tests. None of that nonsense. Dr Berry asked me if I was committed to improving my habits. Dropping some less helpful behaviours and moving in the direction of some better ones. I signed up immediately to six sessions of CBT.

I duly wrote in my journal every night, taking a notebook from the stationery cupboard at work, which was guarded like the crown jewels by our admin worker.

'How many notebooks do you go through in a month, Donna?'

'I do a lot of planning . . . I have a lot of ideas.'

She raised one eyebrow at me, muttering under her breath.

I didn't turn up for the sixth session. I knew it was about endings and avoidance, and it was an obvious and clichéd action on my part. I knew Dr Berry would write that down. I didn't feel too guilty. I was numb from the drugs. Feelings sat outside the bubble. There was happiness, sadness, anger.

I could see the colour of my feelings. Sea green, slate, alizarin. But I couldn't feel them.

I ended up searching for Dr Berry as part of my case against the police, as my notes couldn't be located within my medical records. I found he had moved back to Australia and become a champion ballroom dancer. This felt strangely reassuring.

In the weeks after my drink with Alison I stew on the idea of therapy. Thinking it through into the night, and distracted by it in my own group sessions. I try to impart guidance to the people who've come to me for help. Listen to them, offer words of encouragement. And meanwhile I avoid seeking any formal help myself.

I realise that I am finding my own form of therapy. Writing – my snippets of the past starting to speak my truth. Walking by the sea, focusing on the tiny fragments of sea glass and pottery. I take a bag to collect unusual stones, which will then be used in my group sessions at work. Speaking at trade union conferences and events. Being with the other women, sharing our experiences. This is validation. All of these things have become my therapy.

12

Bobbies and Bath Bombs

Summer 2018 brings a heatwave and the controversial Lush 'Spycops' campaign. The brand has committed to spotlighting the scandal, to urging the politicians to listen to the campaigners. The media attention after my *Newsnight* interview has died down, and by now it has started to feel like the old days. Tireless campaigning, no one listening. But this, attention from a huge brand and company, it feels different. This will spark something bigger. I can feel it in my bones. I have been promised by Mark Constantine, the head of this global company, that he would host our campaign in his shops. And he has been true to his word.

On Valentine's Day earlier that same year Mark had been in the audience as I sat on stage in front of a packed room of Lush staff and celebrities. I was chairing a discussion on undercover policing at the Lush Summit; staff from shops across the world came to this huge expo to launch new products and have a big party. Campaign groups, human rights activists, rock stars; they were all there, filling the room with multicoloured hair, the smell of jasmine, painful-looking piercings and intricate tattoos.

I had been invited along the previous year and gave talks on two separate stages, one with Alison, by then a dear friend, telling our personal stories, and then a session at the invitation of Dave Smith, ostensibly to interview him about his book *Blacklisted*. We were scheduled to go on after the TV presenter and naturalist Chris Packham. We managed to get a couple of photos and Dave gave him a copy of the book.

I got to know some of the senior Lush people at the summit, all of whom had come from an activist background themselves, with a particular focus on animal rights and climate activism. This belief system shaped the model of the whole organisation, from the products to the flat management structure, which was unusual for such a large company. They didn't believe in traditional job titles. It seemed that workers were given a lot of autonomy and if they showed a particular talent, they could easily change jobs.

When the invitations for the February 2018 summit were being sent out, we were all in full activist mode. Tirelessly trying to keep spycops on the agenda, planning events and strategising on how to make maximum impact. It felt like putting Carlo behind me, focusing on something else and having a new role. I didn't want to be the victim any more, I wanted action. I was already plotting how we might present to a bigger audience, in a talk-show format, with me hosting. I imagined I could be like a radical Lorraine Kelly. I would interview Dave plus two of the other women, Alison and Jessica. When I put this to the Lush organisers, they agreed immediately.

On the day of our talk at the summit, the book stage audience was packed, probably due to the hurried announcement that Mark Constantine himself would be introducing us. It was during the Q&A afterwards that Mark made his commitment to a Lush #spycops campaign. Sitting on stage, we were pretty taken aback. This would be a first. A national campaign and one of the biggest retailers in the country highlighting our cause.

The call to action had come from Lush HQ in May 2018. We would have just six weeks to get this campaign off the ground. A time slot for the window campaign had been agreed and as activists we would work in close partnership with the Lush design and media teams to make this concept a reality. Having never done anything like this in my life before, I was excited beyond belief, re-energised. This was an opportunity to test myself, and a means of harnessing my wayward energies. I have always been prone to dips and then upswings in my mood, but having a creative purpose is a salve for me.

Our campaign meetings will be held in Soho, in the stylish Lush studio space, and will include the women in the group and other spycops activists. A short film is being commissioned and a song written and recorded specially for the project. We will be involved in the casting and have editorial input. The first meeting I attend is a heady mix of powerful smells and creative people. I rush home from London on a cloud of patchouli and jasmine, the kids whooping with delight at the goodie bag full of Lush products I was handed on the way out of the door.

At the heart of it will be a striking window campaign, in every store in the UK. The flagship stores, such as Oxford Street, will have enhanced displays, and we will host tailored events and discussions alongside them; we will produce podcasts and new web content, and write media releases and information packs. It is going to be a busy summer.

I am simultaneously putting together a comedy benefit gig, supported by the comedian Rob Newman. It is all going to happen in June/July, advantageous timing for us to raise the profile of our campaign while reaching a whole new audience. One of our main priorities is getting the story of the undercover policing scandal out to the wider public. It currently languishes on the back pages, or on the late-night news.

We have no idea what is about to be unleashed.

*   *   *

When the core designs for the window campaign are signed off by the Lush team and us, the various activist groups, we are delighted. Visually it is stunning. Lengths of blue-and-white tape stating: 'Police Have Crossed the Line'; #spycops 'Paid to Lie' badges; a poster showing a face split in two, half policeman/half activist; postcards that will be signed by customers in shops and which we will then deliver to the home secretary. Then there's the film itself, which is utterly compelling, chilling even. It is quite extraordinary to watch the affable actor transform himself into a sinister undercover spy as the cameras roll. Who would have thought a global company could operate in this way? As I get to know Lush more intimately, I am ever more impressed by the ethics of the organisation. I'm half hoping they might give me a job after this is over.

We produce the podcasts in a recording hub, myself and several of the other women telling our stories, which will then be edited to a professional standard. I arrange a book event at the Lush Soho book club, drafting in Dave Smith, Rob Evans and the ex-undercover policeman turned campaigner and author Neil Woods. It is all going remarkably smoothly.

The campaign is set to launch in shop windows on the morning of 1 June 2018. All shops will set up their window displays the night before and our content on the website will go live at the same time. It coincides with the half-term break and Alison and I secure joint childcare to allow us to be at the flagship Oxford Street store on the day of the launch. Our babysitter will have the kids for a couple of hours and then we can all meet up for lunch.

We meet at Oxford Circus station, beaming at each other from across the crowds. We've met so many times, but this feels different. Celebratory for the first time. The streets are crowded with people and we wend our way towards Lush arm in arm.

It is better than we could have even imagined. A huge photograph, looking out at the passers-by. And people are stopping, looking, considering. We stay there for nearly an hour, thrilled at the exposure.

'Do you think anyone will pick it up?' Alison asks.

'Probably not. But people are seeing it. All over the country!' I respond. We're silent, imagining the people this will reach. The public, that is; we are not expecting much press coverage.

Let's just say it receives a bit more attention than we have anticipated. The boys in blue are not too happy . . .

The backlash really kicks off when a social media account named UK Cop Humour frames the campaign as anti-police while simultaneously calling on their followers to leave bad reviews on the Lush Facebook page. Soon their rating plummets to one star.

Twitter users begin to say they will boycott Lush and by the end of the first day nearly all mentions aimed at Lush's Twitter account negatively reference our campaign.

People are really starting to pay attention. The backlash to the campaign is picked up by the *Daily Mail*, *Evening Standard*, BBC, *Guardian*, *Telegraph*, and every other major newspaper. The phone is non-stop, asking for comments from the women.

Even the home secretary, Sajid Javid, wades into the row with a tweet criticising the campaign. Lush is now getting it from all sides. There is suddenly a boycott hashtag: #FlushLush. My phone is permanently pinging like crazy with tweets and retweets as I manage our social media campaign.

Alison and I start to worry about the impact on sales. Nervously smiling, we agree that it has raised awareness.

'Success?'

'Hmm . . . we'll see.'

Following a number of threats of violence made to their staff by supporters of the police, Lush remove the window displays just six days after they go up, although the campaign was scheduled to run for a month. Shop workers are being intimidated: threatened in store and also outside on the street. A pregnant worker is followed as she leaves at the end of her shift. Lush make a decision to leave the windows blank and make a public statement that the displays have been taken down for the safety of the staff.

For safety reasons, it is decided that our book club/chat-show event will now be private – invitation-only for staff, trusted journalists and activists. They can't risk a public event in the wake of all this inflated fury.

The police call upon their blue-light family, the nurses, the paramedics and the firefighters – for support and I retort in a statement to the newspapers that blue-light solidarity had meant little when the undercover cops were spying on the Fire Brigades Union.

I am asked to write a piece for the Lush website. I am living out my dreams, writing, campaigning and speaking, the old familiar whoosh of adrenalin and the reordering of my scattered brain giving me hyper-focus. Whatever this campaign achieves in the end, I know it has unleashed something else in me. Whatever combination of selves I am, they stand side by side throughout this crazy time. Andrea, my legally assumed name, taken on as a protection against unnecessary intrusion into my private life – the activist who was also a *normal*; Della, my family's nickname, the party girl and extrovert, sometimes inclined to rash decision making; Donna, now living unfulfilled dreams and making new friends around the country. It was like living in a dream state.

The web content stays up and then there is an interesting development. Not only does the campaign receive high-profile support from well-known names, including a letter in the *Guardian* from politicians and journalists, but the police whistle-blower Pete Francis offers his support, as do two ex-wives of officers involved in the scandal. Finally, the son of one of the officers speaks out in support of our campaign. With this unexpected aid it seems the tide might turn, this time in our favour.

We regroup and are told that Lush have decided to run a new window display. It is going to present only facts; just text, no controversial images. It has to be scrutinised by our lawyers to ensure not a word of criticism can fall at our door.

The design goes up on Wednesday, 13 June, a stark white print with black text.

**Over 1,000 campaign groups spied on
by at least 250 undercover police officers.
Infiltrating lives, homes and beds of activists for 50 years.**

I offer a statement to the media, who have been bombarding us with requests for comments:

We're happy that this campaign has drawn so much attention – we have been fighting for years to raise public awareness and Lush has certainly helped to catapult the issue into the public consciousness in a way that we could never have achieved by ourselves.

I read that statement over and over. How lightly it covers the endless fight we've taken on. At last, it feels like we are winning.

I am asked to go on a popular daytime TV show, *Victoria Derbyshire*, to defend the position of the Lush campaign. Convince the general public that what the undercover police did was an abuse of our human rights. My job is to be very normal, engage the audience, encourage empathy. It is scheduled for a Monday morning in early July. I will have to leave home super-early in the morning to catch the train to London. I realise after I agree to do it that I have a ticket for a music festival the night before – Nick Cave and Patti Smith. I will have to curb my behaviour at the gig. It will be fine.

There are calls back and forth for several days about the interview. The BBC decide in their wisdom to invite a police widow onto the show to comment, as well as the usual police commentator, normally a retired senior-ranking officer. The woman's husband died in the line of duty. They are trying to make a horror show out of my story.

'What a ludicrous proposition!' I yell down the phone to Alison, preparing the kids' dinner, rather ineptly chopping cucumber with one hand. 'Trying to pit women against each other! It's not *Jeremy Kyle*, for God's sake.'

'Don't bloody do it! It's exploitative on both counts! Her and you.' Alison has me on speakerphone and I can hear the murmur of her domestic life in the background. She too is making dinner, a more nutritious and thoughtful meal than mine, I imagine. It is Friday night, so she has interesting guests coming round. A well-known crime writer and his wife. I envy the urban lifestyle. I don't have anyone round for dinner these days.

The calls go back and forth all weekend. Finally, at 5 p.m. on Sunday, as I make my way through east London to Victoria Park, I get a call from the Lush media woman, telling me the interview is off.

'Thank fuck for that,' I say, all bravado. 'I'm off to have a pint now.' I call Steve, meet him earlier than planned, regaling him with tales of our exploits and activism. We've grown closer these last few months; he's a friend who knows me, knows what's happening, but isn't deeply enmeshed in this world. Many times I've sat across from him, pouring my heart out. He took me in when I was homeless. He is a constant.

Six hours later, I am attempting to make my way home from London. I've had four more pints and danced furiously around a field. I have sunburn on my chest. The phone rings. Lush, again.

They have agreed to drop the police widow from the show. The interview is on again.

The next morning comes too soon. I am close to retching. A combination of the lack of sleep and too much coffee. Agreeing to go on live TV with one of the top-ten hangovers of all time? I pinch the skin between my thumb and index finger until it stings. *Smart move, you fucking idiot.*

I got home late last night, and before I had a chance to catch my breath I was showered and on my way back to London. I get the bus from St Pancras to the BBC central studios near Oxford Circus, as I can't face the heat of the Underground. The man waving the clipboard under my nose is failing to get me to sign something. A waiver. It is just noise. I haven't taken in any of his words.

They lead me to a green room, a windowless space with a couple of sofas and a hovering make-up woman. I pace up and down, desperate for air. Meanwhile the famous policeman sits calmly in the corner, reading on his phone. Someone comes in and hands me a hoodie. Apparently, my dress is unsuitable for the camera as, at the back, there is a large keyhole of flesh showing at the top. I hadn't really thought this through when I fled the house this morning, running to catch the train after three and a half hours' sleep. I can't wear the dress, I know, but a hoodie?

'I'm a middle-aged woman, for God's sake! I am not going on TV wearing a hoodie! Do you not think that will just perpetuate the *mad activist* cliché? Can you find a black blazer or something? Do you not have a wardrobe department?'

I don't think them supplying me with a smart jacket is too much to ask. They're the BB *fucking* C.

The famous policeman doesn't even look up when I argue with the make-up woman, refusing the white-blond wig she offers. Because it is live TV, they insist I wear a wig in case I am recognisable. I have also been warned not to turn my head in case the camera catches my face. Stupid anonymity order. 'Don't you have anything more natural than this? Maybe a dark-brown wig?' I ask the make-up woman. Off she goes, seething. I sit down, watching the policeman, who remains oblivious.

Will he finally recognise me when we sit down opposite each other in the studio underneath all those lights? Has he in fact already recognised me and is playing a calculated game? They are well-trained liars after all. Should I say something to him? Not now. That would be unethical. Wait. Just wait.

The make-up woman returns with a long brown wig, curled and two-tone in ombre. Dear God. I'll look like a footballer's wife, from the back at least. 'Perfect!' I smile sweetly at her. I don't want to seem like a diva. The producer reappears with a black blazer that he says belongs to one of the TV presenters. It is a size 8 and a very expensive designer brand. I hand it back to him, laughing. 'I'd rip the seams on that!'

Victoria has just been interviewing Grenfell survivors and activists, who return to the green room during the blazer debate. I recognise one of the campaigners.

'Joe!'

My old friend, Joe Batty, the respected campaigner and activist. He's worked in hostels and street outreach like me. I first met him sixteen years before on a supervision training course. We were both about to become managers, me in Camberwell and him in Whitechapel. He was also one of Carlo's best friends and we spent a lot of time together when I was with him. We hadn't seen each other for over a decade. Until now. He looks taken aback to see me.

'What you doing here, Donna?'

'I'm just about to be interviewed by Vic Derbyshire wearing this terrible wig, but I need to find a bloody jacket! My dress has a big gap with my flesh showing at the back and it won't look good on the camera.' I turn around to show him.

Huge hugs are then forthcoming. Joe is wearing a smart cardigan over his stripy shirt, bottle green, pure new wool.

'Would you lend me your cardigan?' I touch his arm, full of cheek.

'Aye, of course, you can have it.'

'I was joking, sweetheart.'

'No, seriously . . . take it.' He already has the cardigan off and is pressing it into my hands.

My anxiety has settled. Perhaps it is Joe's steady presence, or the dopamine release triggered by his bear hug. Or his cardigan, secure as a baby's comfort blanket. I'm ready now for a grilling from Vic Derbyshire and the famous policeman, who still hasn't looked up from his Twitter feed.

I feel confident as we walk to the studio, calm as I sit down across from Vic, next to the famous policeman. He is remarkably civil, engaged from the moment the cameras roll. He says he disagrees with the Lush campaign and trots out the familiar 'only a few rogue officers' line. He then completely decries the behaviour of the undercover officers in the SDS, including Carlo. I get the last word in, about institutional sexism in the police and how I am still experiencing obfuscation in my civil case, despite the police accepting liability two and a half years before.

The filming ends neatly, and we make our way back to the green room. I decide to seize my chance.

'Excuse me, could I have a word? In private?' I direct this to the famous policeman.

He looks surprised but nods his agreement. I usher him to a small room next door that I've spotted is empty.

He looks at me quizzically.

'Do you remember me?' I ask quietly.

'No . . . should I?' He looks worried.

'We've met before. In Greenwich. I managed the drug treatment service there. I'm Donna, in real life.'

'Oh my God!' He holds his hands up to his face. 'It's you!' Suddenly it has come back to him. 'You saved my life, you know.' He puts his hand on my shoulder. I think he might cry. 'Yes, your service saved my life.'

Soon after my rough-edged TV appearance, the Secret Spycop's Ball is upon us. Rob Newman has chosen the title and enlisted his friends Mark Steel and Stewart Lee to appear on stage with him at this comedy benefit gig. I planned it with him, in the café at the British Library, accompanied by Alison and Helen Steel. I did my very best to appear calm.

I'd last seen Rob Newman in the flesh from a crowd when I lived in Edinburgh, back in 1993, when he was a rock-star comedian. He and his then comedy partner David Baddiel were the first stand-ups to perform to a crowd of 12,000 at Wembley Arena. The rock-star life didn't suit Rob, who was fiercely intelligent yet a remarkably gentle character, and soon after I had seen him in the nineties he made a departure from the world of showbiz, choosing instead to devote his time to writing novels and engaging in political activism. He was involved with the environmental group Reclaim the Streets, which is how he and Helen came to be friends. At one of our Police Spies Out of Lives strategy meetings early in 2018 we had discussed fundraising ideas and a comedy benefit seemed a good option. Helen introduced me to Rob and suggested I take over organising the gig, as she was busy with her own stuff. What a turn my life had taken.

The Secret Spycop's Ball in July 2018 hasn't been planned to coincide with the Lush #spycops campaign; however, the furore that ensued over the poster campaign in early June has meant that I have to reassure the worried venue manager that there won't be any protests or disruption against us, and that the staff will be safe. As well as Rob, Mark and Stewart – arguably three of the most successful comedians in the country – we also now have a brilliant up-and-coming stand-up called Evelyn Mok on the bill. Tickets sold out on the day they were released, but we have been given a generous quantity of complementary tickets for our group.

After the stress of the Lush campaign, this is to be a bit of light relief. The women are travelling to London from all over the country and our lawyer Harriet is coming too. There are a few spares for our activist friends. It's going to be a fantastic night for everyone. Except possibly me.

I have been asked by Rob to do a short speech during the show. He is compèring as well as doing his own set, and he is to introduce me onto the stage. While my friends chat and have drinks in the bar, I am in the girls' green room with Evelyn, alternating between pacing back and forth, reciting my lines under my breath and applying more eyeliner. Next door in the boys' green room, the three famous comedians seem hugely relaxed. Stewart Lee is eating a takeaway straight from the foil container and Mark Steel has just arrived, having been held up after a cricket match.

I am to be introduced by Rob after the interval, so I will be on just before Mark Steel. Jesus.

Standing offstage, I can't believe how dark it is. I've rehearsed walking on five times already. I'm wearing Birkenstock sandals as it is such a hot day, but now I'm worried they are either going to fall off or I'll trip over them.

'Should I go on stage in my bare feet?' I whisper to Evelyn, 'or will that just reinforce to the audience that I'm a mad hippy?' She tells me to put my shoes on, with a wink.

Rob gives a short introduction on the history of undercover policing and the relevance of our campaign: my cue to join him on stage. The audience applauds. And breathe.

I walk towards the microphone, hands gripped tightly behind my back as they are shaking so much. My notes are held there too, rigid between my fingers, a mere prop now. I look to the last row of the audience where my friends are, but it is shrouded in darkness. I can, though, hear Alison and Jessica whooping loudly.

'Thank you, Rob. My name is Andrea. This is a pseudonym, as I have a court order to protect my anonymity.

'On a beautiful sunny day in September 2002, on an anti-war demonstration, I met a handsome activist and we fell madly in love . . .'

I look down at the front row and see my friend Liz, her big smile and halo of blonde hair gleaming up at me. She managed a sister drug service when I worked in London, and we've spent many years talking through what we've seen, sharing laughs. I beam back at her and continue my story.

The audience is silent as I tell them how Carlo, the locksmith, moved in with me after six weeks, how he proposed on Hogmanay and how he met all of my family and friends, and came to our most intimate gatherings. I explain how things began to change and after a traumatic revelation of family abuse he exhibited signs of a breakdown, disappearing for days at a time, even threatening suicide.

Occasionally I hear a sharp gasp, an intake of breath in response to some shocking part of my story.

I want to finish with something funny, to lighten the mood again.

'As some of you might be aware, a certain high-street company, most famous for its sweet-smelling bath bombs, has been getting a bit of bad press for supporting our campaign. I have a wee story to tell you about that . . . In the early nineties when I lived in Edinburgh my flatmate had two obsessions in life. One was Rob Newman, who I'm standing here with today. The other was a small company from Poole called Cosmetics to Go, started by a certain Mark Constantine. That company was the first iteration of Lush. Little did I know that twenty years later I'd be standing here on a stage at Jacksons Lane, talking to you about the Lush spycops campaign, in the company of none other than Mr Rob Newman himself!'

Applause. Pause.

'Thank you all so much for coming along and supporting our campaign. Please follow the hashtag #spycops to find out more. Now back to the comedy.'

I do a small, awkward namaste bow and noisily clump offstage in my sandals, tuning in to the loud whoops from my comrades at the back of the theatre, to be greeted with a hug from Mark Steel. An experience and a half.

At the end of the gig, I make my way downstairs to the front of the theatre, trying to catch Liz after spotting her from the stage People are not moving and I suddenly realise it's because there's a queue of people waiting to speak to me. An Irish activist I've met before at a conference, some complete strangers, and one of the theatre's sound engineers. There's a young dreadlocked man, who holds out a copy of the programme and asks for my autograph.

It feels intrusive and I just want to get back to my friends. But I chat politely, answering their questions, although as succinctly as I can, not wanting to get caught up in this public reminiscence.

'When did you first suspect something was wrong?' asks the sound engineer.

'I don't know, it's hard to pinpoint exactly. Possibly when we arranged a holiday to France and he cancelled it the night before.'

13

Nothing Lasts Forever

Everything had changed after that summer of 2003. We never made it to France. Or anywhere else. Carlo began to tell me stories about his childhood, divulging them over wine in the evening. He was drinking more than usual. He looked at me as intensely as ever and held me just as tightly, but something was different. His eyes? More shadowed? He grew a full beard, which made him look older than the neat goatee had. His hair had grown out, becoming scruffy, and the bald patch on the back was more obvious. But no – it was his smell. I began to think his smell changed. How could that be explained? Toxic shame? Untruths?

Carlo said his father had been violent, handy with his big fists. Fists that looked a lot like his own. He said he felt guilty, dirty. Tarnished. Ashamed that he hadn't protected his mother.

'You were only a child, I said.' I tried my best to reassure him. I shared my own stories. My father was small and wiry, a typical wee Scottish hard man who liked a drink or twelve and would turn on you like a terrier. Carlo heard my stories and we shared our trauma, but we differed on shame. I felt none, at least not in relation to any of this. In him, the shame was so firmly rooted that it was capable of suddenly etching hard lines on his beautiful smooth skin. I felt more helpless than I was willing to accept.

*　　*　　*

Carlo spent that Christmas in Italy. We had agreed that he would travel back to me on New Year's Eve. Hogmanay. The anniversary of the marriage proposal.

At the last minute he rang me. 'I've decided to stay, as my dad's condition has worsened.'

Not long left, they said, best not to leave yet.

I rang in the bells of 2004 with Lucy, Dan and a few quiet socialists at a house party in Walthamstow. There was no lucky coal to be found in E17. I was worn out with it all. I sat listlessly in the conservatory, beside the gas heater, while Lucy smoked Dunhill Lights out of the door. I played with the teardrop pendant on the necklace Carlo had bought me, unable to concentrate on the conversations around me. I was restless and fidgety as I waited for the phone to ring, missing Carlo and wishing I was at home in Scotland instead of here.

At 3 a.m. on New Year's Day Carlo rang to say his father had died.

'Do you want me to come?' I asked. I already knew the answer.

'No, there's really no point, darlin'. You've never met any of them and Italy's a long way. I'll be home as soon as it's over.'

He confirmed the distance between us. This life of his I wasn't part of. It felt like it was getting further away. The wedding was rarely talked about these days. No more Sunday-afternoon discussions in the pub by the canal, scribbling down playlists for our first dance or working out a mixture of menus for the carnivores and the vegetarians. No more seating plans; two Italians, two Scots and two from the London gang at each table.

At 4 a.m. Lucy and I wandered through the east London streets trying to find a taxi, arms linked together in solidarity against the misery and the cold. I realised I had nothing in the house for our New Year's Day dinner. My mum would be appalled. She and my sister would be having a traditional steak pie from Hood's, the butchers at Prestwick Cross. There would be Ayrshire potatoes and buttered carrots, just like every year. They would wash it down with a wee Advocaat and lemonade and toast the memory of our granny. I hated steak pie, but I missed my granny. I missed her and I missed Carlo and life felt too vast and unknown to be comfortable.

When Carlo finally came home two weeks later, he didn't look the same. He had lost weight. His eyes truly were different. As soon as he walked in through the door I knew that something catastrophic had happened at the funeral. He didn't touch me, recoiling, holding his hand out as if to demarcate the distance between us.

It happened after the funeral, he said. His sister disclosed that she had been sexually abused by their father. From age eleven. She'd held this secret for twenty-eight years.

'I need time, Donna. I need time to sort myself out.' He couldn't look me in the eye. 'I'm going to stay with Steve for a couple of weeks, just to clear my head.'

I realised that now I couldn't smell him. It was gone. The familiarity of his scent had disappeared. I knew then that I was losing him.

A clammy wave of shame washed over me, nausea rising and then settling in my gut like turned milk.

On the day of the move to Camberwell, Carlo was distant, distracted. He stayed over that night but didn't seem comfortable in Matt's newly decorated, pristinely tidy flat. He didn't even want to eat out. We had unpacked some basics and stacked the other boxes neatly in the corner of my room.

Shower sex, floor sex, all of it was empty of feeling and my heart was heavy from the weight of knowing it was going nowhere. It all stank of unhappy endings.

I handed Carlo a bottle of prosecco to open, which Matt had left in the fridge – a welcome gift.

There had been a 'happy new home' card waiting for me atop the pine chest of drawers:

To Della,
Glad you're coming to live with me. We'll have fun galore!
Sparkly in the fridge for you.
Lots of love honey xxx

He was in Milton Keynes for the weekend, visiting his new boyfriend.

'Food?' I sat on the edge of my new bed, dragging my tights back up my thighs in preparation for going out.

'Let's just phone for a takeaway.'

'Really? There's loads of good food places round here. Thai, Vietnamese, Laotian?' I was suspicious; the man loved food and eating out in new places was one of his favourite things.

'No, I'd prefer to just stay in tonight, darlin', I'm whacked. Can you just ring up a pizza place?'

He handed me my glass, oddly jumpy and hyper-alert; for some reason he just didn't seem comfortable in south London.

'This doesn't look like you,' he said, surveying the very clean beige room.

'It will be fine once I put my books out and get my prints up on the walls, it will de-beige a bit . . .' I smiled. 'I've read this now.' I pointed to *The Reader,* which protruded from the top of a leather weekend bag.

'What did you think?'

'So much loss, and pain. Secrets. I couldn't put it down.'

The next time Carlo came to the flat was a couple of weeks later. Matt was positively bristling. Carlo spoke with faux politeness, lacking any of his usual humour. Matt was abrupt and avoided eye contact. Unsurprisingly, thanks to his rudeness, Carlo eventually left.

'Are you *seriously* asking me why I don't like him?' Matt spluttered.

'Yes!' I was seething, giving Matt my evil eye.

'You mean I need another reason, apart from the fact that he treats you like shit and uses you for sex?'

'Well . . . yes, that's my fucking choice!' I reddened in shame. That was so below the belt.

'He has taken advantage of you, kept you hanging on because you love him. And he's a homophobe!'

'What? Carlo is many arsehole things, but he's not a bloody homophobe!'

'You better believe it, honey. He is.' Matt looked at me, stony-faced. 'I can smell it.'

The last time I ever saw Carlo was late on a Thursday night, outside Regent Street Cinema. We went to a long Italian film about the breakdown of a marriage, told backwards. When we left the cinema, he walked ahead and flagged down a taxi.

'Camberwell, please, mate.' He held the door open for me, the distance between us widening to a chasm.

'I thought I was coming back to yours.' That was the routine. Knickers and toothbrush stuffed in my handbag under my work notebook.

He faced me and then handed over a wad of notes to the driver. 'Here you go, mate.' Then he turned and walked off.

I sank into the car, avoiding the gaze of the taxi driver. I guessed what he was thinking and it wasn't pleasant.

From: minesaducati@gmail.com
To: DonnaMcLean@TR.org

12 November 2004

I am writing to say goodbye for the last time. I have tried, but I can't make it work. I have to move on now. I'm sorry to hurt you. I loved you more than you will ever know.
Carlo

An envelope arrived two weeks later. The sight of his handwriting made my stomach churn with fear, hope, promise, loss. It contained a note saying he would always love me and a gift voucher for the Sanctuary Spa in Covent Garden. A full day of spa and treatments, lunch and a glass of champagne. And a gift box to take away.

'That would have cost a small fortune!' Matt raised his perfect eyebrows, grabbing the card out of my hands.

'It's going straight in the bin.' I gripped onto it, resisting him.

'Don't be ridiculous! What a waste. Give it to someone for Christmas, honey. Do a raffle at work for the clients. I would use it, if it wasn't women only— Come here,' he said, seeing my crestfallen face, and gave me a teddy-bear hug. 'Now forget about that homophobic bastard. He really is no good.'

I never heard from Carlo again. Once, a couple of years later in 2006, I believed that I saw him. I was on the Underground, travelling across London to a drugs policy conference in Kensington. A large, dark man sat opposite me, brown eyes, big hands, soft lips. So familiar, but he had long straggly hair under his baseball cap and a biker jacket with band logos sewn on. It was disconcerting to see someone so similar yet so different. It couldn't possibly be him, I reasoned. An acquaintance told me he was in Italy now and he certainly hadn't developed a penchant for German death metal. I was deluded in thinking otherwise.

14

Intrusion

From October 2018, I am jumpy, anxious and very easily startled by noises. I feel panicky in the dark and when travelling on trains; the latter I have to do regularly for work. Around this time, on one occasion I feel that someone is following me as I am walking back from the station to my house. In hindsight this was not the case but because of my heightened sense of risk during this time, I perceived that it was. The feeling of being followed, and the feeling of imagining you are being followed, have the same results on your nerves.

While I try to pull the threads of my psyche together, the investigation is unspooling around me. My case is moving forward well, according to Harriet. The public attention around the undercover cops is greater, the demand for real retribution. The pressure on the police is intensifying, and they know it.

It is fairly early in that October, the ninth, that I attend an ABE interview with the police at Folkestone police station, followed a week later by an assessment by Professor Sweeney, a psychiatrist instructed by the Metropolitan Police. That assessment takes place on 15 October 2018 at the Maudsley Hospital in London. Both of these events are seared on my memory. Both will have a significant impact on my mental health. Both are, apparently, within the ask of the Met.

* * *

The ABE interview is a clinical examination of my relationship with Carlo that takes three hours. The ABE – 'Achieving Best Evidence' – interview is a format for questioning victims of rape/ sexual assault. I received a letter, a short, formal note explaining the process and giving the details of when the interview would take place. It didn't say, in any great detail, why I would be required to do it. I called Harriet, who explained that it was part of the process if I wanted to proceed with a criminal case against Carlo. She said they needed as much detail at their end as they could get. For their own 'investigation' into what they had, themselves, condoned.

Folkestone police station is a sprawling, grey, ominous building. A sixties slab that from the outside looks impenetrable. They treat me kindly, make me a cup of coffee and show me to an interview room. Years of crime dramas rush past me, and I eye the mirrored wall warily.

The interviewers, two female detectives from the Metropolitan Police, are not aggressive in their questioning of me but it is a very difficult and stressful experience due to the intimate nature of the questions. I've told my story so many times, but for the most part it has been about the relationship, the stretch of time, the shift from love to absence. This is different, this is every single detail. I find it distressing at times, particularly when recounting in detail the child sexual abuse that Carlo told me had happened in his family. He had come home from Italy, towards the end, a broken man. He'd told me a terrible 'truth' he'd found out at the heart of his family. He was shaken, desolate, and I would have done anything to support him. He had told me of the sexual acts that had allegedly taken place, including anal and oral rape. He told me it started when she was eleven. Sitting on a ripped plastic sofa in this grim interview room, I am hit with the realisation that all of the stories were made up. They were invented by Carlo, first to get my empathy and then to form the foundations of his exit strategy. In this cold room I feel my insides start to churn and my eyes well up. I feel like something is stuck in my gut and I am scared I'm going to vomit in front of the policewoman. My logical brain understands that just about everything that took place in this relationship was a lie, but I haven't processed what that really means. I haven't allowed myself to feel. I've been in survival mode. I haven't had to deal with the emotions of it. Until now. I am psychologically laid bare, my vulnerabilities naked under the harsh yellow strip lights.

The detective asks me about our sex life. How often, where, what were his preferences? Did we use contraception?

'Not condoms,' I said. 'I was on the pill. We were in a monogamous relationship.' She looks at me pointedly, but I can't read what she is saying. Is she judging me? Sympathising with me for being so seriously duped?

'His wife . . .' I say, shaking my head. Thinking about how she was pregnant while we were together. Thinking about how he wanted me to get pregnant. Did he seriously want to have two children born within weeks of each other? This whole thing is insane.

'He didn't care about either of us.'

The detectives smile gently at me, move on to the next question. And the next, and the next. Those three hours feel like three days, and no amount of coffee and conciliatory words make it easier. I leave shaking, head towards the sea, walk in the salt air until it clears my head. I go home, don't mention it. Carry on.

*　　*　　*

A week later I am obliged to attend another psychiatric assessment the Met have insisted on, at the Maudsley Hospital in Camberwell, south London. I used to work across the road and many of my street homeless clients had been patients there. The clinical psychologist I saw in 2005, Dr Berry, was based there. This one is not just a doctor, he's a professor, a senior forensic consultant who specialises in working with mentally ill offenders. I do not want to do this. I feel angry and resentful that they are forcing me to. I haven't recovered from the last psychological grilling and my skin feels too thin for any more prodding. I look up the professor, trying to find any slurs, smears or complaints against him. I discover he was the psychiatrist for a man who was killed in police custody in Brixton police station. I vaguely know the family, through our joint campaigning with the family justice activists.

When the eight women in the previous case against the police settled their claims they had also seen Dr Clifton, an independent expert in complex trauma who was instructed by our lawyers to report on the impact of the deceptive relationships. I found her to be clear and sensitive in her approach. None of the other women had been forced to see a psychiatrist appointed by the police. The Met are refusing to progress further with my case until I attend an assessment with their expert. I am furious on three counts: one, I am being forced to undergo this violation; two, I am being forced to see a man and they refuse to allocate a female psychiatrist; three, he is a forensic shrink, not an expert in trauma.

I call Harriet, my solicitor, and plead with her to find a way of not having to do this. She explains that I don't have much recourse here, that it is simply within their rights to ask. It doesn't make any difference that to me it feels like an intimidation tactic, a device to force acquiescence to power. I want them to know the impact it will have on me, but even if they did understand I don't imagine they'd care.

'I think I will crack this time,' I say, my voice trembling. 'Can't we just refuse?'

'They won't progress your case if we refuse, Donna. You have to do it if you want to reach a settlement.'

I am stuck between the devil and the crossroads, but I have no soul to sell. I am godless.

Excavating the bones of your life over and over again is re-traumatising. In the lead-up to the assessment I feel an anxious, heavy dread. I have the added ugly promise of night terrors to look forward to. Vivid nightmares, in which I am about to die at the hand of an unseen assailant. Sometimes there is sleep paralysis, the incubus, where I feel I am awake but am paralysed as the horror descends on me, crushing my body. My screams are silent. Eventually I wake, and I am screaming. I am soaked in sweat. I am unable to move for a few minutes, shivering in the cold as my brain processes reality versus my dream state.

The time finally comes for the interview that I have been dreading so much. I am booked for the very end of the day. I sit in the dark waiting area, people around me either too high or too low. No equilibrium to be found within this space. I pull my hastily bought turquoise cardigan tightly around my body. I left home with the sun shining and arrived in London to a hailstorm. Nothing but grey skies.

A small man in a petrol-blue suit comes into the reception area and calls my name.

'Miss McLean?'

He was supposed to use my pseudonym.

He was supposed to use my pseudonym. This name I've been

carrying around. My children call me Mum, my family and friends call me Donna. But for several years I've also been 'Andrea'. A 'victim', a 'survivor', an 'activist'. It's hard to explain the fragmentation of being called something else, the strangeness of creating an identity for this other woman. Is she stronger than me? Or more fragile? Funnier, warmer, weaker? I am still trying to work it out.

'It's Andrea,' I mutter, following him over to a side room adjacent to the main reception area.

This room is nothing like Dr Clifton's therapy space. It is institutionally ugly. There is a floor fan right beside my chair that is obscuring my view of the professor and an overflowing bin at my feet. I move them both behind the chair, without asking.

The professor doesn't offer me a glass of water, so I take my own bottle out of my bag, only to realise it is leaking everywhere. I must not have screwed the top on properly when I got off the train. There is water all over my jeans now, a wet patch right in my groin, as if I have peed myself.

Professor Sweeney is an angular man with a downturned mouth and a steely expression. He smiles thinly at me as I come in, beckoning me wordlessly to the armchair. And so I recount it all again, an articulate robot. Yes, this happened; no, I'm not suicidal. Yes, I love my children dearly and they're the best thing to ever happen, but sometimes I feel absent, not always the best parent. No, I haven't self-harmed or deliberately made myself vomit since I was a teenager. Yes, I did have multiple intrusive thoughts of a sexual nature following the discovery that Carlo was an undercover police officer.

I am forced to go back to all the childhood shit again. Domestic violence. That was the bond between us. Childhood trauma.

Why must I keep saying it? It does not matter any more. I cannot muster any more fight. I am almost defeated. They are winning.

I leave the Maudsley in a fugue, and head straight for the bar beside the station. I order a large glass of dry white wine and head outside to the benches overlooking the train tracks. I play with my phone, opening the contacts and wondering if I should call someone to meet up. My friend Iain lives just down the road. My Spanish friend is two minutes away. Mike is nearby. But I decide not to. Why would I dump this toxic emotional waste on anyone else? I feel dirty from the debris that has been shaken loose during the session. I fear I will start to scare people away. Best not to call anyone.

'They've broken you,' says one of the others in the group. We are at a legal meeting, but she keeps trying to drag me aside, to interrogate me about my most recent psychiatric assessment. She is desperately trying to avoid having to undergo an additional assessment herself, the last one having affected her so badly. She had to retreat for a while. No emails or phone calls to her, our solicitor instructed.

'You've been through the same,' I said, and we sat in silence for a minute or so.

She tells me that she felt close to breaking when the police wrote requesting she go through another assessment.

'Why,' I ask, 'what else do they need?'

'Nothing. They've got it all.' We both know they want to break her spirit, like they have mine. We all know this tactic of being assessed by the opposition is designed to put off other women who have been similarly deceived from suing the police. There is a tsunami of new cases about to emerge. The public inquiry is now informing new women that they have found through the secret files, and an increase in public awareness means that other women who suspect they had a relationship with an undercover officer are seeking legal advice. We've talked about it, our lawyers trying to prevent these assessments, but nothing has changed it. They can do what they want. It's nothing personal, they keep telling me. My lawyers, my barrister, my friends.

In the days and weeks after my ABE and Professor Sweeney interviews I became heightened, sleepless, agitated and distracted. I was distant from my family, racked by guilt but incapable of preventing it. All I wanted was to protect my children, especially after months of emotional absence, where they had suffered the impact of these events on me. They were the great light that brought me out of the cloud after Carlo left. Now the tentacles of his lies were reaching into our home.

I became reactive, snappy and easily drawn in to arguments. I'd pace my hometown, head down but waiting to bump into someone, for a car to beep at me, for something that would let me release some of the pain. It wasn't like me. I hated to watch myself acting like this. Then the nightmares came, like clock-work; always of a similar nature, they involved someone in my house, something threatening, a presence I cannot see but that I know seeks to do me harm. When I wasn't having nightmares, it was because I wasn't asleep, lying in bed panicking, insomnia taking over.

In those weeks I pulled back from everyone: Helen, Alison, the men. The support bubble who'd wrapped around me, who'd made me feel like what I'd experienced was terrible, but also something I'd get over. I answered the odd call, responded to emails, but I no longer made the trip to London for a university talk or a trade union conference. I wasn't in the mood for laughing, sharing stories over a drink, reminiscing and planning. But without all this, I felt at sea.

As I hung onto my family life with my fingertips, my work fell apart. The impact of the interviews on my work performance was frightening. I work in the field of mental health and I teach mindfulness. On one occasion in November 2018, during a session I was teaching, I had my eyes closed and suddenly Carlo's face was there. This had never happened before, and really scared me. When I opened my eyes I felt he was still there, in a physical sense; I could smell him. It was an intense and horrible experience and stayed with me for days, making me feel scared, anxious and ashamed. I also had a number of episodes of intrusive thoughts of a sexual nature; I recalled the physical experiences I had with Carlo. These thoughts were a real challenge to deal with; I felt vulnerable, guilty and ashamed and had a sense of losing control.

A few days after the appointment with the professor I trip and fall into a hole in the road. My foot gets stuck at an awkward angle and I twist my knee. Black and purple bruises map my body like dead flowers. I am the wounded woman.

My dogs recognise my wounds, both physical and psychological. I love my dogs. They lift me out of myself more than anything or anyone. Their legs are short and their jaws are strong. They catch grouse, pigeons, dogfish, rabbits. They don't kill their prey, just ensnare the petrified beasts in their mouths and then bring them to me, as a gift. I screeched like a banshee the first time a live grouse was deposited at my feet, but you get used to these things. You get used to anything.

And what about Carlo – did he even like dogs? We were going to have a dog named Che, plus our three children.

He said he had a dog named Eva, a pointer, when he was a child. Or was it Ava?

He said Eva was a great truffle-hunter and she was stolen for her talents.

Eva was also his mother's name. His mother who was violently beaten by his father, he of the big fists.

Was any of this true? Or was this just another way to manipulate me?

To mirror my feelings?

To distort reality?

To make me love him?

He knew how much I loved dogs.

Christmas passes in a blur of flu. I struggle to get to Scotland for the new year. My mum and sister have gone overboard on presents, worry pulsating out of them. They fuss around me, care for the girls, carry out a charade of cheerfulness as I spend days in bed, feverish and agitated in the daytime by the visceral sense of my nightmares. 2018 passes to 2019 and as I clink whisky glasses with my family I think back on that Hogmanay when Carlo proposed. All I can see is the strange look he threw back at me before disappearing into a bedroom with some of the men.

In January my lawyer calls, tells me gently that they would like to arrange a second consultation with the psychologist, Dr Clifton. She needs to speak to me again. I want to say no, but some small voice tells me to go along.

I make the journey on autopilot, to the station, on the

train, through London streets to Dr Clifton's office. I sit across from her, the room warm, comforting, so different from Professor Sweeney's. She smiles at me, asks how things have been since we last spoke.

'I've had intermittent periods of heightened anxiety, panic, insomnia, lack of concentration, feeling like I might pass out, tightness in my chest, feeling like I am choking.'

I list the incidents that trigger the anxiety, trying to get the dates in the right order.

'When I was followed across London after being in court, it really freaked me out. Someone stood behind me as I waited for a tube at Westminster. I had seen him staring at me outside the high court, and then he popped up hours later in a different part of London. I must sound mad.'

She says no, I don't sound mad at all, that it must have been terribly frightening.

'Having the rape interview, as I call it. That was hideous. In a horrible, smelly police station. It stank of skunk. The police-woman was okay, but it was being video-recorded and there was someone watching in another room. The questions were highly intrusive. I had to describe what he looked like naked. His body hair. His funny-shaped toes. His penis. I mean, Jesus Christ! After all that I found out the CPS wouldn't prosecute. All of that, for nothing!!'

She asks what happened, and I have to explain that after everything, laying myself bare, the Crown Prosecution Service made a blanket statement on all our cases, to put all the other women off making complaints. There would be no prosecutions for sexual offences due to genuine feelings. Genuine feelings. They are trying to excuse Carlo by saying he really loved me. He wasn't even real. It is yet another deflating, denigrating experience and highlights in the most basic way how institutionally sexist the criminal justice system is. Consent means nothing.

Dr Clifton is sympathetic, though I'm sure she's heard this sort of story so many times. Sitting across from women let down by the CPS, left to recover alone. She asks me to carry on.

'Waiting for the report from their expert, the professor. It took four months when he said it would take two weeks to complete. Oh, and seeing him in the first place. That triggered a whole episode, one of the worst. I had a flashback at work. I couldn't get the image out of my head. That threw me completely. Even when this was taking over every bit of my life, work was always a safe place. Then I fell in a hole in the road and bruised myself from head to toe. Literally got stuck in hole.'

I know I'm talking too quickly, letting out a rush of things that don't quite fit together. I can feel my face flushed, my heart beating fast.

'So, what would you say has helped?' Her question makes me pause. Dr Clifton wants to know how I managed to get through all this. I'm also wondering how I have got through it all, but I realise that I have. I am still here, even if I feel like I've been taken apart like a Rubik's cube and put back together in the wrong sequence.

'Walking the dogs by the sea, writing, spending time with the other women. Keeping my head above water, talking about it. Making sure people know how huge this scandal really is. Not being broken. I won't be broken.'

She tells me I'm not broken, and puts her pen down, the main part of the interview over. 'Your solicitors are keen to get my report as soon as possible. It sounds as though they are close to settling your case.'

'Finally! It's only been four years!' I laugh. 'This really has derailed my life.'

She smiles at the understatement. Asks, 'Do you think you'll drop your anonymity at some point?'

As she asks it, a feeling rushes through me. Something like hope, or power. 'Absolutely. It's exhausting. It's hard work being two people.'

Having a pseudonym and keeping my story secret is akin to being in witness protection, it is meant to keep you safe but feels like a loss of personal freedom. In that moment, sitting across from Dr Clifton, I realise how much I want to be Donna, not Andrea. It needs to be dumped now. I have decided that I no longer want a false identity, that it doesn't feel protective. This double life was forced on me by Carlo's deception. I am not ashamed of who I am. I want to stand in my own truth, in my own name.

15

Secret Agents and Provocateurs

My vignettes about my life with and without Carlo started to add up to quite a pile of pages. Back in December 2016, Dave Smith encouraged me to write a newspaper article on spycops. It was published in a journal called *Union News* in early 2017. My first published piece since I was at school. I joined Kerry Ryan's local creative writing course, Write Like a Grrl, at the same time and this outpouring of life writing began to flow. Kerry, taken aback by the content, encouraged me to keep writing at the end of the six-week course.

Late in 2018 I was accepted by Penguin Random House to join their mentoring programme for disadvantaged writers. I applied spontaneously, having seen a post about the competition on Twitter. The application process was in four stages, and I was convinced at each that I would receive a polite email saying I hadn't made it through. But I did. I received the final yes while I was manning the chocolate fountain at the school Christmas fair.

I had written a few more articles in the mainstream press and had a short story published in a literary magazine by the time I started working on my book with the support of Helena Gonda, an editor at Penguin's imprint Transworld Books. I was tentatively starting to think of myself as a writer, although I wouldn't say it out loud. Not yet.

*   *   *

The award-winning journalist has arranged to meet me in the Quaker Meeting House on the Euston Road, as I am there already for a meeting. He initially suggested the pub. We have been introduced over messaging by a mutual friend, one of the activist researchers I have known right from the beginning of this saga. He has been wanting to speak to me for months, but I kept putting it off. At this stage I am tired of talking to journalists. I need to write my own story, not keep on telling it to other people. But then this journalist released Carlo's real name to the world, in a single tweet. I feel the need to meet this man. He's not scared.

I tell Alison beforehand. She sounds a note of caution. 'He's very charming. It's a great way of getting information from you.' In the end, curiosity gets the better of her and she stays for this meeting too.

I appraise him as he climbs the stairs toward us: early fifties, silver-fox hair, crisp white shirt and a classic black leather jacket, with an expensive messenger bag thrown over his shoulder. Someone does his laundry, I think. He sits down, facing Alison, across the imposing oak table that dominates the upstairs hall in the Quaker Meeting House. We've been using it as a rather sophisticated and free meeting space for our campaign.

The journalist and Alison have not seen each other for almost a decade. There is a palpable spark between them. He is overtly charming; they reminisce about the last time they met and she twiddles a tuft of hair. I watch and listen, waiting for a cue to speak.

Finally, he turns to look at me.

'Hi. At last we get to meet.' Hand outstretched.

'So, what do you need from me?' I ask, slightly exasperated now. Their fond catching-up is very sweet, but it is taking up my precious time. I need to get home to feed the kids and walk the dogs. Bluntness is necessary with this one.

'I want to hear your story.'

'I've already told it, it's been on the telly twice, and in *countless* newspapers. I'm actually writing it myself – a memoir.'

He looks surprised, then very quickly hides it. 'Brillian,' he says.

Of course, I have googled him before we met. This is par for the course now. Investigate the investigators. I learn that he had a price on his head at one point and had to go into hiding, after doing an exposé of a well-known gangster who had half the Met Police in his substantial pocket. I had not paid a great deal of attention to the story at the time, but now follow anything to do with police corruption much more intently, given the connections with our stories. Our spycop boyfriends were intrinsically linked to the blacklisting scandal, keeping men like my mates Dave and Steve and Liam out of work for decades. The police were feeding information about trade union activists to many of the big building firms, who paid £2.50 per name on the illegal blacklist.

In the Stephen Lawrence case, not only were the police complicit in letting the murderers go free, they went on to spy on the grieving family and tried to discredit them with a campaign of lies. It has since transpired that there were links between the investigating team and a team of south-London gangsters. The layers of corruption run deep. If I think about it too much it becomes uncomfortable. In a small way, just like the award-winning journalist, I am also taking on the state and its deeply embedded corruption. I am just an ordinary person, a small-town girl, but I am sticking my head above the parapet and shouting about institutional sexism, racism and police abuse.

What risks might this entail? After the incident of being followed I am certain that I am still under some form of surveillance.

On one occasion recently, I checked my social media logins and found that my Facebook account had seven different devices in Bury St Edmunds. I had never been to Bury St Edmunds. But the name did ring a bell. I remembered seeing on the news that the Anonymous activist hacker Lauri Love's computers were taken to the police IT HQ at Bury St Edmunds. Some people might think I'm crazy, but I am not. Nor am I paranoid. This level of intrusive surveillance is real. If the British state will infiltrate your life to the extent of inhabiting your home, your bed and your body, of course it will hack into your digital world. When I think about this reality, I am aware of an ever-present sense of unease, a physical discomfort that is buried deep in my gut, at least during the daytime. At night it plays out in nightmares, where my uncertainties and fears become a vivid stage for the macabre.

The journalist begins naming some of the police he knows well – the good guys, so he says – reeling off both familiar and unfamiliar names. Convincing me of his credentials before he starts fishing for information.

'Have you met Frank Matthews?'

'Not in real life, no. We've only ever chatted on Twitter. Mainly about book festivals.'

He's one of the good ones.

I knew Frank had been an undercover officer, working on organised crime and corruption. He turned whistle-blower due to the racism he witnessed in his department. Like the award-winning journalist, Frank was unpopular with the Organised Crime Groups and had been put in witness protection at one point. The officers from Special Branch who were meant to be protecting him from the OCGs turned out to be corrupt. You really couldn't make this stuff up.

'It's surreal that we've ended up crossing paths with all these characters. Like *Line of Duty* but worse in real life.'

Alison giggles. The journo looks over at her, eyes dissuading her from distracting me. We smile at our shared in-joke. The strangest conversations happen in Twitter land, with the most unexpected people, especially when you have an anonymity order.

'And Peter Bleksley? Do you know him?'

'Oh yes, I've met him.' I glance over at Alison again. 'We were on the Victoria Derbyshire show together, at the height of the Lush furore. He wasn't too unkind to me, all things considered.' I don't let on about the previous encounter I'd had with 'Blecks' in my real life, back in 2006.

'He's very much one of the good guys.'

I don't want to talk about him, as that forces my different worlds to collide. I mention another ex-cop, who I've spoken to several times.

'So you must know Neil Woods then? He was an ex-under-cover in the drug squad? He seems to be on our side.'

Alison nods at me.

'He's been to court a few times for inquiry hearings, and he was really supportive during the Lush campaign.'

The journalist shakes his head no.

'He seems decent,' I say. 'I had read his books before all this started. He is an activist now, against the war on drugs. And his wife, she came along to the last inquiry hearings too. It was the time we went for lunch in the Patisserie Valerie opposite the Royal Courts of Justice and that red-faced, fat-necked cop kept staring at us, do you remember?'

'The bald one I asked to move away from us, you mean?' Alison laughs and turns to the journalist. 'I always ask them to move to the seats on the other side of the courtroom. Those bastards don't intimidate me.'

I rub my neck and shoulders, shifting my position on the hard wooden bench. My muscles are tight and knotted, about to trigger another tension headache. 'God, these seats are uncomfortable.'

'I think that's our cue to depart to the pub,' says the journalist, looking at his watch. 'We can talk more there.' He turns to Alison. 'You coming along?'

'Oh God, no, I need to get home for the kids.' She wraps her light green scarf around her neck. 'Another time.'

'What about you, Donna?'

'Why not? I've got time for one.' Four o'clock. Sod it, I can get the next train home. I still don't know exactly what this man wants from me, much as he has thrown me a crumb or two.

I divulge to him all about the horrific psychiatric assessment at the Maudsley and the potential criminal investigations of undercovers, which have been written off by the CPS. I tell him about the trip to Bologna to see the site of the train station bombing. We end up agreeing a visit to the deli owned by Carlo's sister, as well as a potential doorstepping in the Home Counties. I think I must be losing the run of myself. Control slipping out of my fingers once more.

'Would you like to see him again?' he asks me over our last drink.

'Yes, absolutely. For a while I was reluctant. I might not know if he was telling the truth. Now I'm convinced that he's a sociopath, so I would never believe a word that came out of his mouth. But I do want to see his face now. I want him out of the shadows of my imagination. I want to see him exactly as he is: fat, bald, middle-aged. Riding around on a midlife-crisis motorbike. Fucking retired on medical grounds at the age of fifty-one!! Bollocks to that. They set up the whole thing. He *conveniently* retired just before I made a criminal complaint. But they "forgot" to tell me and let me go through a rape interview. Which was pointless, because they had already let him go. Found him not guilty of any misconduct, despite having already accepted liability for my case. It stinks. Bastards.'

'They conducted a rape interview?' He doesn't understand what I mean, this serious revelation appearing among a cascade of swear words and venom.

'Yes, it's exactly how they would conduct a rape interview. Forensic questioning. Horrible. Really distressing. It set me off again.' I shiver at the thought of it all, pulling my coat tightly around my chest. 'The psychiatric assessments and the interviews dredge up everything. I don't sleep so well, get edgy.'

When I rush out of the Euston pub, overly hot, I am a bit giddy from a pint and a half of Birra Moretti. The chat has been engaging and I let my guard down as the alcohol kicked in, the tension in my neck loosening as well as my tongue. I feel a slight crawl of fear over my skin. I've said too much. As usual. Too trusting. Logic tells me he isn't going to write any of this down. My stuff is personal, emotional. He's not a tabloid journalist, for God's sake. His interest is in police corruption, sniffing it out and exposing it. My inner world has no place in the article he will write about Carlo.

He wants to expose Carlo as an agent provocateur. Like Bob Lambert before him, Carlo is accused by activists of attempting to incite arson, another firebombing incident. Another attempt by the police to try to frame innocent people and cause a miscarriage of justice. It's sinister and it makes my blood run cold when I think what the consequences could have been.

My engagement was a hoax, my whole relationship a scam. I was well and truly duped. His tears were never real, they were crocodile tears, born out of manipulation.

The night the firebombing incident was suggested was Hogmanay and it suddenly hits me, like a fist in my face. Now I know why he asked me to marry him on that night. It was to distract me and the other women there, the other girlfriends. When he took the boys off to the bedroom for a chat, when he turned back to me with that strange look, he was actually plotting an arson attack.

16

The Women

'Think of the first room you ever remember. Recall the sensations you experienced: what you saw, smelled, heard, what you felt and tasted.'

I am in a light, spacious room, overlooking a calm sea. Kefi Chadwick, the successful playwright and our writing mentor, is encouraging us all to do a warm-up exercise to lead us into writing our stories. I am fidgety and want to get on with my own work. I don't need these exercises; the words are already bursting to get out of me, pent up and frustrated, having been forced to stay in my head for so long.

The idea of holding a writing retreat for all of the women had come to Alison and me during the Lush campaign. We were on stage in the Lush studio in Soho, holding the books about spycops written by our friends Dave and Rob. I announced that one of us should write our own book. Currently our stories were written by men. *We are going to write our own anthology.* Later that year we raised the funds for a weekend campaign and writing retreat. We were going to Aberystwyth.

Fifteen of us travel to the Welsh seaside, making our way from all over the country. We will use this space to write our own stories.

Alison, Helen, Rosa, Lisa, Belinda, Jane. This is the original group of women, where the story all started. Lisa had uncovered Mark Kennedy back in 2011, just as Rosa was approaching

Helen Steel to confirm the devastating news that her missing partner was in fact an undercover officer. Alison had been searching for her missing partner, Mark, at the same time, convinced that he was a state spy. A mutual friend put her in touch with Helen.

Monica, Jessica, Lindsey. New friends. They began their legal cases against the police just after me.

Lindsey had a relationship with Carlo before I met him. She had been introduced by a mutual friend and they were together for almost a year. He was evasive about why the relationship ended. Carlo took her to Venice on holiday and bought her an expensive camera for her birthday. She took superb, moody pictures of him, including the infamous photo used for Conrad Landin's 'Spycop accused of incitement to bombing' story in the *Morning Star*. There was a short gap, around three months, between the relationship with Lindsey ending and the relationship with me beginning. Like me, Lindsey is a socialist and trade unionist. Like me, she is working class (from Liverpool). Like me, she has long hair and loves art and photography. We skirted around each other a bit in the beginning. Who knows what he said, what lies he told, what distortions he wove into their conversations? Lindsey is warm, kind, smart and funny. We have become good friends. I bet Carlo hates this.

Monica and I first met in between our initial psychological assessments. We had our appointments with Dr Clifton booked in on the same day. Harriet Wistrich had put us in touch via email. I had of course run over on my appointment by an hour, and Dr Clifton had to call Monica to let her know. When I finally got out, tear-stained and smelling of spilt coffee, we managed to meet for ten minutes in a café next door to the therapy rooms. We recognised each other instantly, despite never having set eyes on each other before. As with my first meeting with Alison, I believe the instant recognition comes from that unique sense of shared experience, our eyes locking together to discharge some of that fear and tension that built up prior to our psychological testing.

Monica has long black hair in a style not dissimilar to my own. She is a creative. In our writing room in Aberystwyth, I look at all of us as a group. There are so many similarities. Creative, therapeutic, articulate, empathic women. Many of the others in the group are highly educated. I don't fall into that category, but I had a relatively successful career when I met Carlo. I wonder if the undercover cops had designed a profile for the women they would go on to target, a sort of prototypical activist. Five foot six, long dark hair, curvy, educated, maybe one tattoo, must love animals.

Jessica was deceived into a relationship when she was young, just nineteen, by Andy Coles (brother of Reverend Richard Coles). Coles was thirty-two but pretended to be twenty-four. He was, like all of them, married with children. Jessica is darkly funny, immensely kind and she has a particularly sharp sense of comedy timing. She has been vegan since her teens, and I reckon that is why she looks so young. She also has long dark hair, which is extraordinarily shiny.

'Did you rinse your hair in vinegar this morning, Jessie?'

'What are you talking about, Della?' She always calls me by my nickname.

'My granny told me that was a trick for shiny hair! And she made me wash my face outside in the morning dew on May Day every year.'

'My God, Della, you were probably washing your face in cats' piss!'

Jessica was an animal rights activist in south London when Coles infiltrated the group and targeted her. She has a rescue parrot that goes mad whenever Rob Evans from the *Guardian* is on the phone. We always laugh about how our paths would never have crossed except for this bizarre connection that first brought us together on Valentine's Day 2018.

Jessica has become close friends with Rosa, who lives in Wales. Rosa is one of the original eight women who took a case against the police. She is an ethereal and fiercely intelligent presence in the group. She was in a relationship for nine years with a man she thought was a fellow activist.

He disappeared, apparently experiencing a mental health breakdown. Rosa searched for him for a year and a half after he went missing. During that time, he emailed her 'clues' and warned her not to speak to anyone. Then one day he reappeared, turning up at Rosa's workplace. Within two weeks of his reappearance, Rosa was pregnant.

He isolated her from her friends, and the relationship became increasingly controlling and abusive. Eventually, Rosa escaped to a women's refuge with her children. We now know of four women who had children with undercover officers, and we believe there are many more.

Maya and Bea have come along to the writing retreat having only just met on the train. They have both only recently found out that they too were deceived into a long-term relationship with a police officer. Both were contacted by old friends who had seen a name released by the public inquiry.

Maya is a PhD student. She is younger than most of us, shy and incredibly beautiful. We met for the first time just a few weeks ago, in our regular haunt, the café at the British Library. She only recently found out that the man she had thought of as the love of her life lied about his identity. The man she fell in love with, who wrote her love letters for years, and who promised her a house and children, was in fact an undercover cop. He disappeared, then five years later came back and promised her the earth, and so she left a five-year relationship. He disappeared again six months later.

Bea is confident and assertive. She discovered recently that her one-time partner, who she met when she was a single parent with a young child, was a Special Branch officer. He is the only black undercover police officer within the Special Demonstration Squad that we are aware of. It appears that he spied on Stephen Lawrence's family.

Maya and Bea instantly join our exclusive spycops survivors' club, where bonds form quickly and humour is dark.

All the women here at the writing retreat bring something unique and yet we are all connected, like constellations. Despite our different ages, backgrounds, religions, political traditions, we have a strength in common. It is a solidarity of understanding.

We would travel miles to support each other, and we often do. We are sisters. We have a responsibility to each other, to be truthful, to be vulnerable, to share our experiences. It is an uncommon bond.

I introduce the structure of the weekend to the assembled group. As well as Kefi, we have support from Kerry Ryan, who is now a friend as well as an experienced writing tutor. The women will only work with people who are recommended by someone in the group, for reasons of safety and privacy.

Kefi, Kerry and I have agreed that we will split into two groups; the original eight plus me as a token extra, and the newer group. Kefi will lead the first one and Kerry will take the second. Our task over these two days will be to choose a particular aspect of our story and draw it out. As we are aiming to create an anthology, we want different bits of the spycops story to be highlighted.

Our group heads upstairs to use two light, bright workspaces overlooking the sea. Kefi will meet with each of us for a one-to-one over the weekend. This group has some accomplished writers in it. Alison has been published widely in the national press and has completed the Faber writing course. Her novel is almost finished. Helen Steel has written numerous articles and papers and of course she has a brilliant legal mind, having represented herself against McDonald's in the McLibel case.

I sit beside Kerry on the train home. Several of us are travelling to London and then on to our homes, scattered around the country. Kerry is exhausted but it's also apparent that she has enjoyed this weekend.

'What a huge privilege to be involved. Everyone has been fantastic. The quality of the writing is astonishing.' She wrinkles up her nose and smiles, red lipstick immaculate as always.

'I'm so pleased you could come! Everyone loves you!' I smile. 'You know I would not be writing a book if it wasn't for you.'

'Ach, don't be daft! It's your story, hen. You were always going to write it. You just needed to find your voice.'

I think back to December 2016, when Dave Smith asked me to write a newspaper article on spycops. I remember how scared I was. Scared of humiliating myself. Scared of not being good enough. I anxiously sent it off and then waited for the inevitable edits to be sent back. When the editor responded, he said it was great and he had not changed a single word. I joined Kerry's course a couple of months later and it felt like I had come home.

I realised writing was my therapy, just as it had been when I was a child. I realised then that I had found a way to cope, a way to process the absolute madness of the spycops story and my peculiar part in it.

I have found my voice.

EPILOGUE

Owning My Truth

I have come to believe over and over again that what is most important to me must be spoken, made verbal and shared, even at the risk of having it bruised or misunderstood.

Audre Lorde

In July 2020, after five years of living a double life, I drop my pseudonym. I've been known as Andrea when I've talked in public and in published articles. Initially a protective measure, as I was concerned about the privacy of my work and family life, it has gradually become a hindrance. At a conference in November 2019 a friend accidentally called me Donna on the stage. Someone tutted at him and he replied, 'It's the worst-kept secret since Clark Kent and Superman!'

I made a decision then that it was time for Andrea to go.

I decide to tell my children the story, as I hope they are now able to comprehend this part of my life. They are remarkably pragmatic, if initially shocked. They chastise me for lying about 'where all the Lush bath bombs had come from'.

The response to becoming myself again has been warm and receptive. I no longer lie about my job at the school gate or mislead the neighbours as to where I have been for the night (film premiere rather than training at a mental health service). Lying to people daily was exhausting and unhealthy. I am no longer split between two worlds. It was hard work, like carrying a rucksack full of unwanted rubbish you have accumulated over the years. It needed to be dumped. I did not want a false identity. This double life was forced on me by Carlo's deception.

I am unashamed and I can stand in my own truth. There is no facade, no front, no indignation, no comedy, no chat-show host persona to hide behind.

Last year, at the height of the pandemic, I left an abusive relationship. It had been affectionate for the nine months that I was pregnant. For the other thirteen years his approach to me could be plotted on a graph somewhere between patronising disdain and outright violence.

This is an ending of sorts. Shortly afterwards I settled my case against the Metropolitan Police. I was awarded damages and given a full apology.

But at the end of the day, it's just me, me and my story, hoping to survive, to be not too bruised or too misunderstood.

This book has been my companion through the hardest times. I've escaped the outside world to write my story, to expel demons, to try to understand the incomprehensible.

Ultimately, it has saved me.

Thank You...

To my brilliant agent, Gordon Wise at Curtis Brown. For wit and wisdom, being the best in the biz and having my back during the toughest of times.

To my wonderful editor, Harriet Poland at Hodder Studio. For championing my book, editing with the most intuitive touch, listening (a lot) and for believing in me.

To the amazing team at Hodder Studio, for making the book a reality:

Assistant Editor – Bea Fitzgerald

Publicist – Emma Knight

Marketing – Alice Morley

Production manager – Matthew Everett

Audio – Dominic Gribben

Artwork – Aaron Munday

To Niall Harman at Curtis Brown, for being exceptionally organised and kind in response to my scatty emails about contracts and the rest.

To the three astonishingly talented humans who encouraged me to start this whole adventure: Kerry Ryan, Dave Smith and Kefi Chadwick.

To my writer gang, for sharing time and skills, and for generosity and support all along the way: Lauren Aitchison, Lisette

Auton, Astra Bloom, Rachel Burns, Barbara Byar, Jacki Hall, Laura Kay, Annie Kirby, Priya O'Shea.

To Helena Gonda at Transworld, for mentoring and friend-ship on the Penguin WriteNow programme.

To the Arts Council of England, for the DYCP grant which gave me the time and scope to write.

To my comrades at Police Spies Out of Lives. A peerless peer support group and the smartest women you could ever hope to meet. Could not have made it through this crazy maze without their strength and wisdom. Proud and humbled to stand beside them.

To all those in the wider activist/ researcher support network, for their courage and solidarity: Blacklist Support Group, COPS, Undercover Research Group, Tom Fowler, Rob Evans, Phil Chamberlain.

To my legal team. If you're going to take on the Metropolitan Police, it really helps to have the best people in your corner: Harriet Wistrich, Sarah McSherry, Phillippa Kaufman, Nick Brown.

To my family: my mum Anne, sister Laura and stepdad Alex. For years of love, listening, belief and hours of free childcare. And to my beloved granny, Bridget, who lives on in our hearts and in our actions.

To my good friends: Jo, Kirsty, Rowan, Tania, Amanda, Celia, Euan, Steve. To the memory of Alison, who we miss so much.

To my love, Mick. For hope, trust and poetic synchronicity every single day.

To my girls, Saoirse and Rosa. For making my world shine. This book is for you two. Stay fierce and stay kind.